D0732218

Little Dose of Laughter

CROSSWORDS

CHALLENGES WITH A BIT OF HUMOR

Inspired by Faith

Little Dose of Laughter Crosswords
©Product Concept Mfg., Inc.

Little Dose of Laughter Crosswords
ISBN 978-0-9914172-0-9
Published by Product Concept Mfg., Inc.
2175 N. Academy Circle #200, Colorado Springs, CO 80909

Written and Compiled by Patricia Mitchell
in association with Product Concept Mfg., Inc.

All scripture quotations are from the King James version
of the Bible unless otherwise noted.

Scriptures taken from the Holy Bible,
New International Version®, NIV®.
Copyright © 1973, 1978, 1984 by Biblica, Inc.™
Used by permission of Zondervan.
All rights reserved worldwide.
www.zondervan.com

Sayings not having a credit listed are contributed by writers
for Product Concept Mfg., Inc. or in a rare case,
the author is unknown.

Little Dose of Laughter

CROSSWORDS

Laughter is like a blessing that tickles from the inside out.

This is more than just a crossword puzzle book—it's much more! *Little Dose of Laughter Crosswords* brings you a plethora of fun puns, witty quips, and clever cartoons to add a little humor to your day. Each puzzle is designed to amuse you, entertain you, and get your puzzle-solving gears a-going.

Ready, set, go—let *Little Dose of Laughter Crosswords* tickle your brain and your funny bone—and most of all, enjoy!

Did you hear about the chicken that
walked into a restaurant?
"We don't serve poultry," the manager said.
"That's okay," replied the chicken.
"All I want is a cup of coffee."

Let's Get Moving!

Hurry and see how many action words you can catch with the
clues provided.

ACROSS

2 Greet the morning. (2 words)
7 Play a role.
8 Use you "engine ears" and you'll
   __ a train in the distance.
10 What the judge was asked
    to do? (2 words)
13 Call of the riled?
14 Get down to earth?
15 You can do it if you find the key.
16 Go a mile in someone's shoes.
19 Don't forget to do it!
23 Heart's part.
24 Put on a wet coat?
25 Pen a letter or send an email.
26 Get back on your bike?
28 Complainer's choice with
    cheese?
29 Deliver a punch line.

DOWN

1 How the boat shows affection
  for the shore. (2 words)

3 Weekend activity.
4 What the vain woman did when
  she found a gray hair.
5 Dog's garment?
6 Do it on the driveway.
8 Apathetic owl couldn't give one.
9 Snag your stocking?
11 Lawyers lose them sometimes.
12 What the math teacher told
   her class? (2 words)
16 Pancake with nonskid surface?
17 What you can't do to a boiled
   egg. (2 words)
18 Get new upholstery for the
   old chair?
19 What the duck said to his
   creditor? (2 words)
20 Get on the road.
21 Car owner's need, maybe?
22 Best month for going forward.
27 What the chess-playing
   banker said?

7

As They Say...

Try your hand at these wacky takes on familiar sayings and witticisms.

ACROSS

1 If at first you don't __,
   you're about average.

4 With a smile as your __,
   you'll get a mouthful of rain.

6 A __ excuse is better than none.

7 If you're seeing __, it doesn't
   mean it's springtime.

9 __ is what you pay for maturity.

11 "Yes!" on action words?

12 A penny saved is __. (2 words)

17 If you can't stand the heat,
    get a __.

18 Opportunities always look __
    going than coming.

20 Rusty workshop cutter...or a
    saying you've heard time and
    again! (2 words)

21 Never underestimate the power
    of __.

22 You can't teach an old dog
    new __.

23 Doesn't matter whether you
    win or lose--until you __.

25 One good turn gets most of
    the __.

27 The other line moves __ until
    you get in it.

28 Those who throw dirt always
    lose __.

29 In our 24/7, interconnected
    world, "no news is __!"

DOWN

1 A journey of a thousand miles
   begins when someone says,
   "I know a __".

2 Don't bite the hand that
   looks __.

3 If something can go __, it will.

4 Remember, you're __, just like
   everyone else.

5 If everything's coming your way,
   you're in the wrong __.

8 It's a small world, but you
   wouldn't want to __ it.

10 A diplomat is one who thinks
    twice before saying __.

13 Life is full of __--or is it?

14 Change is good, but __ are best.

15 Female parent's saying?

16 You can't have __--where would
    you put it?

17 Where there's smoke,
    there's __.

19 __ while the bug is close.

24 __: A good walk ruined.

26 He who __ last didn't get
    the joke.

A proverb is a short sentence based on long experience.
Miguel de Cervantes

Across

1. SUCCEED
4. UMBRELLA
6. LOOK
9. AGE
11. PROVERBS
12. NOT MUCH

Two cows saw a milk truck pass by the pasture. On the truck's side was written, "Homogenized, Pasteurized, Vitamins A & D added." One cow sighed and said, "Kind of makes you feel inadequate, doesn't it?"

Noah's Ark

Big or small, furry or feathered, see how many creatures you can name!

ACROSS

1 He's always on the web!
4 Time-keeping critter? (2 words)
6 You can't help but notice their colorful details!
7 Errand-runners?
11 Mom with her brood in a snood?
13 Spiny critter takes the whole bush?
14 They have a lot of pride.
16 Don't get hiss-terical if you see one!
17 They're forever bragging!
19 Poultry across the road?
20 You don't want them to quack-up.
21 Is a group of them called a wig?
25 Give them oinkment when they're sick.
26 "The __ stops here."
27 They're quite sluggish without their shells.
28 Boring insect?
30 Can these insects spell?

DOWN

2 They're always wearing trunks.
3 Do they have hindsight?
5 It grows down as it grows up!
8 Don't fall in one when it's raining!
9 They love knock-knock jokes.
10 They're usually in school!
12 You've got to be kidding!
15 Throat-dwelling critters?
18 He's a real stinker.
21 Stable animal?
22 They look hoppy, don't they?
23 Pasture bullies?
24 Crafty pond swimmer?
27 Ram-bunctious ones?
29 You might get a kick out of one.

Oops!

"The baseball mania has run its course. It has no future as a professional endeavor."

Cincinnati Gazette editorial, written in 1879

Batter Up!

You shouldn't strike out on any of these clues!

ACROSS

2 Hunk of coal?
5 Dad.
7 Players on each team.
9 "You're it!"
10 Cave dweller?
11 Toddler's paradise?
15 Hand holder.
16 Not a home game. (2 words)
17 Foundation?
18 Stocking snag?
19 Zoo scene.
22 Whacker.
23 Moon lander?
24 Win or lose?
26 Official, for short.
28 Fan's seat.

DOWN

1 "Hooray for us!"
3 Gopher's work.
4 "Who can swat this thing?" (2 words)
5 Kitchen need?
6 Black as __.
8 No-no.
11 Theft?
12 Temptation to miss work. (2 words)
13 Group.
14 Not working today?
16 Look at the weather! (2 words)
20 Spaceman's grass?
21 Fan's snack-in-a-bun.
23 Baseball letters.
25 Lemonade stand need?
27 Squeeze-y batter?

Little Susie watched her mother apply cold cream to her face. After a few minutes, she asked, "Why are you doing that, Mommy?" "To make myself look beautiful, darling." Then Susie's mom picked up a tissue and started wiping off her face. Seeing this, the child said in amazement, "Mom, are you giving up so soon?"

Lookin' Good!

It's all about beauty in this puzzle!

ACROSS

1 Halo wearer.
6 Beauty salon.
8 Hair style for a burger?
9 Romance in a fish tank? (2 words)
10 Mouth pole?
12 Sharp curve.
14 Breakfast makeup?
16 Rooster's crown.
19 Powder, for short.
20 Bristly character.
22 Olympic slider?
23 Apiarist's do?
24 Who's the fairest of them all?
25 So's the salad!
27 Rouge, and shy person.
29 Egoists' delight?
30 Beauty contest.
31 Curling tubes.

DOWN

2 It's done for looks.
3 Town cutup?
4 Robert's fastener? (2 words)
5 Magnet's response to beauty? (2 words)
7 What she did when she saw gray.
9 Is it set yet?
11 It only indicates where smiles have been.
13 Fragrance.
15 DIY tools?
17 You get one in an elevator. (2 words)
18 Chilly skin-smoother? (2 words)
21 Farmer's response to beauty? (3 words)
26 Symbols of beauty (stop and smell them).
28 What the feline flatterer could be doing?

Mel: "I got hit in the head with a soda can!"
Sal: "Oh, that's awful! Does it hurt?"
Mel: "No, I was lucky—it was a soft drink."

Thirst Quenchers

Settle in with a nice cold drink—
How many of these can you get, do you think?

ACROSS

1 Mush gush.
4 Electrical selection?
7 Recipe direction.
10 Cranapple, for instance.
11 Chill!
12 Some like it this way.
13 What a drip!
14 Orange or lemon.
17 Beverage to have during an earthquake?
18 Cap it & carry it.
19 Thirst-quencher in the limelight?
21 Pass the __, lass!
24 Are you able to find this container?
25 Take it in.
27 Here's looking at you!
28 Guilty pleasure, maybe.

DOWN

1 Just a little, now.
2 Lumpless liquid.
3 Saucer's mate.
5 Mull it over first.
6 Breakfast beverage.
7 Get a loada this one!
8 Pour me some, too, please!
9 Cinnamon, maybe.
10 Soup stock.
15 Choose long ones for ice tea.
16 It comes on tap.
20 Cool yule beverage.
22 "Hay there!"
23 Beverage go-with.
26 It comes at a steep price!
27 Udder choice?

17

A boy went into a pet store and asked the clerk for a quarter's worth of birdseed.
Taken aback at this strange request, the clerk said, "How many birds do you have?"
"None yet," the boy replied, "but I'm hoping to grow some."

Spread Your Wings!

Spread your wings, because you're sure to light on the answers!

ACROSS

3 It watches...and watches.
4 She might be a mother.
5 Baseball lover's bird, maybe.
6 It can't fly in New Zealand... or elsewhere.
8 Peaceful bird.
10 House bird.
12 It might be afraid...very afraid.
14 Leggy one.
19 This little bird isn't sad, is he?
22 Speedy flier.
23 They have songs.
24 You want a cracker, you say?
27 Another baseball fan's bird.
32 Can you sing like one?
33 How crazy are they, anyway?
34 You won't regret omitting an R.
35 Field hunter, smallest of 22 across.

DOWN

1 It's what you do when you eat.
2 It won't take you up on a dare.
7 Feathered friend.
9 It's noted for its eyesight.
11 "Nevermore" bird.
13 How fast is it?
15 Feathered alarm clock.
16 Water wader.
17 A country.
18 It's not pretty.
20 "Watch out for that falling piano!"
21 It might bore you.
25 Farmer's smart bird. (2 words)
26 It wouldn't flinch, would it?
28 How dumb is it?
29 They'll honk at you.
30 This bird is known to follow a whim.
31 No strings attached on this one!

With great reverence, a little boy opened the family Bible that always sat on the living room table. As he was carefully turning the pages, a big leaf slipped out and fell to the floor. He picked it up and studied it. "Mom!" he shouted, "I think I just found Adam's clothes!"

Treasured Titles

Take a stroll through the library with this puzzle.

ACROSS

1 Jane Austen's meddling heroine.
3 __ Earth, Pearl S. Buck.
5 Mary Shelley's monster.
7 Of __ and Men, John Steinbeck.
11 Robinson __, Daniel Defoe.
12 Wuthering __, Emily Bronte.
14 __ of Darkness, Joseph Conrad.
18 Treasure __,
   Robert Louis Stevenson.
21 A Christmas __,
   Charles Dickens.
22 Herman Melville's whale
   of a tale. (2 words)
24 Black __, Anna Sewell.
26 Henry David Thoreau's pond.
27 Sherlock __,
   Arthur Conan Doyle.
29 Toni Morrison's cherished one.
30 F. Scott Fitzgerald's great one.
31 Robert Louis Stevenson.

DOWN

1 Around the World in __,
   Jules Verne. (2 words)
2 __ of Monte Cristo,
   Alexandre Dumas.
4 __ Copperfield, Charles Dickens.
6 Lord of the __, William Golding.
8 Time __, H. G. Wells.
9 __ Letter, Nathaniel Hawthorne.
10 Call of the __, Jack London.
13 Adventures of __,
   Mark Twain. (2 words)
15 War and __, Leo Tolstoy.
16 The Good Book.
17 __ Book, Rudyard Kipling.
19 Pilgrim's __, John Bunyan.
20 The __ of Dorian Gray,
   Oscar Wilde.
23 Homer's long journey.
25 Secret __, F. H. Burnett's.
28 Gone with the __,
   Margaret Mitchell.

THE SHORTEST DISTANCE BETWEEN TWO POINTS...
IS USUALLY UNDER CONSTRUCTION.

Road Signs

Check out this "bumper crop" of pithy sayings!

ACROSS

3 Don't __–I'm pedaling as fast as I can.

4 If you can read this, I've lost my __.

7 On the other hand, you have different __.

10 There's no __ in time travel.

12 Of everything I've lost, I miss my __ the most.

13 Blink! Use your __ signals.

14 Corduroy __ make headlines!

17 Gone __; back soon.

18 Driver cleverly disguised as a responsible __.

19 He who laughs __, thinks slowest.

21 Be __! The world needs more lerts.

23 If everything is coming your way, you're in the wrong __.

24 __ is what keeps everything from happening at once.

26 No matter where you go, you're __.

27 I used to have a __ on life, but it broke.

DOWN

1 I'm serious–it was a __.

2 In theory, everything __.

4 A bicycle can't stand alone; it's two __.

5 I may be left-handed, but I'm always __!

6 __ is inevitable; suffering is optional.

8 Change a life; make someone feel __.

9 It's been __ all week.

10 My other car's bumper sticker is actually __.

11 Never, never, never, never __.

15 When the going gets tough, the tough go __.

16 __ is inevitable, except from vending machines.

17 If you lived in a __, you'd be home by now.

20 Warning: I __ for yard sales.

22 Don't __–it's paid for.

24 Ever stop to __, then forget to start again?

25 Do not __! This car is part of a dirt test.

26 Drive defensively–buy a __.

The only thing you get that's free of charge is a dead battery.

Rev Up!

Some of these clues might come *auto*matically!

ACROSS

1 Clunker.
7 Convertible.
8 Carry-all.
11 Honkers.
13 It might be stretched.
14 Semi section.
16 It's between you and
   the sidewalk.
18 Speed reader?
19 Toothy wheel.
20 Go-anywhere goer.
22 It's tracking behind.
26 They might be heads or tails.
28 It's under the hood.
31 Weekend wheels.
32 Watch it!

DOWN

2 Coolant conductor.
3 Road most traveled.
4 Lawn-lover's love.
5 Oinker on the street? (2 words)
6 Odometer reading.
9 It's always behind.
10 It's on a course. (2 words)
12 It's in a hurry. (2 words)
15 It's big!
17 Stop!
21 Don't drive it on the tarmac!
23 Right or left?
24 Go, go, go!
25 Four-door.
27 They're coming 'round.
29 Station stop.
30 Stay in yours!

A beleaguered police dispatcher received a phone call. "I've lost my cat" the woman cried, "and I need you to help me find her." The dispatcher sighed. "We really can't help you with that today, because..." "Oh, but you must," the woman interrupted. "You see, she's a really intelligent cat. She can even talk!" "Well then," the dispatcher said. "Perhaps we'd better hang up right now, because I'm sure she's trying to call you."

It's the Cat's Pajamas

You're sure to solve this one *purrr*fectly!

ACROSS

3 Noted cat characteristic.
5 Face feelers.
6 "He's a __ cat, up-to-date with everything!"
8 Fancy car?
10 "Is it a secret, or is the cat out of the __?"
11 Box fill.
12 Cat covering.
13 You might be smitten with one.
15 "She's a real glamour __!"
16 Hello!
17 Mane cat?
20 This cat's wild!
21 Not on the sofa, please!
23 "Hey, quiet one, cat got your __?"
24 Male cat.
25 "You look great! You're the cat's __!"
26 Big cat's little one.

DOWN

1 Contented cat's sound.
2 "Those two fight like cats and __!"
4 Double-dealing cat?
6 "Keeping this group together is like __ cats!"
7 Claw-holder.
9 Member of cat family.
10 Persian or Siamese.
12 Cuddly cat's name, maybe.
14 Food favorite.
16 Cat's nemesis, by tradition.
18 Treat.
19 Cats take a lot of them.
21 Patch's patches.
22 Multi-colored cat.
24 Striped cat.

CHRISTMAS is a time... when hearts are filled with love, homes are filled with laughter, and jars are filled with COOKIES!

Ho Ho Ho!

Have a jolly time solving this puzzle!

ACROSS

3 Jar fillers.
4 You might pine for one.
6 Eastern shiner.
8 Christmas surprise for kids.
10 Last-minute prep time.
11 "The First" of song.
15 "__ Night."
16 Not one was stirring.
17 Christmas list category.
20 Bah, humbug! man.
23 Pre-Christmas activity.
24 One half of the list might get some!
25 Bows partners.
27 Seasonal ride.
28 It's that time of year.
29 List category.
30 Nutty slice of Christmas?

DOWN

1 "Jingle __."
2 "O Little Town of __."
3 Pole treat. (2 words)
5 Burnett, Lawrence, Channing...
7 27 Across pullers.
9 Proclaimed "Glory to God in the highest."
12 Mantel dangler.
13 Seasonal log.
14 Old flames?
18 Season's greetings.
19 They're around the table.
21 Jolly one's entry point.
22 Christmas bloomer.
26 Christmas circle?
27 "Let it __!"

29

"Honey, the phone is still ringing. You're answering the remote control."

Yakety-Yak

Here's a puzzle everyone can talk about!

ACROSS

1 Field communication.
6 Walk the __.
7 Quiet communication.
9 Modern cafe.
11 Communication with no strings attached?
13 You hope it's free.
14 Handy communication, for short.
15 Video call enabler.
16 Your grandmother's phone choice.
17 It's not paper anymore.
18 Introduce yourself! Show me your __. (2 words)
19 Intelligent phone.
20 "That was funny!"
22 Smiley face.
24 Hand-held electronic apparatus.
27 Phone message.
28 Beeper.
29 Space for everyone to join in.

DOWN

2 "You mean there was a time when you didn't have __??"
3 Find a long lost relative, perhaps.
4 "Yes, that's what I said…"
5 A mouse does it.
8 __ networking site.
10 Morse code device.
12 __ service, communication via Teletype.
15 Lofty communicator.
18 Elements of communication.
19 Camper's signals.
21 Phone choice.
23 Wordy space. (2 words)
25 Lettered letter?
26 Unwanted communication.

A college freshman walked up to his roommate and said, "I got us a cookbook so we can cook some of our own food. Trouble is, we can't make any of the recipes." "Why not?" inquired the roommate. "Are they all really complicated?" "No," the freshman replied. "It's just that they all start out with the same thing: 'Take a clean bowl.'"

What's Cooking?

Nibble at this puzzle until the whole thing's well done!

ACROSS

4 You'll have to ask a lot of questions about this one!
6 Get that liquid bubbling hot!
7 Game piece.
8 Where it all happens.
11 Little-girl ingredient.
12 Load mine, please!
13 Shapely dish.
15 Make butter.
16 All-in-good-fun tribute?
18 Dip partner.
19 Table shaker.
20 Baseball figure?
21 Strip the cheese!
22 Lane game?
23 Fix whatever ailed the ham?
24 Get it preserved.
25 Big cooker.
26 Make it crispy!

DOWN

1 Add volume.
2 It's not a dark secret how to do this!
3 Bones-be-gone!
4 Sidewalk covering?
5 Use your rod and reel!
9 Morning bread.
10 Get it together, please.
14 Cookie maker.
15 It's also known as leftovers.
16 Some cooks follow it.
17 How sweet it is!
21 Let off __.
23 Do it on the cutting board.
25 Ado?

33

Sally's idea of a balanced diet is a chocolate cookie in each hand!

Just Desserts

This one is sure to sweeten your day!

ACROSS

2 This answer has many layers.
6 Chaotic dessert?
7 Fido's favorite, for sure!
10 Creamy confection.
12 No need to fiddle with the facts!
14 It made the apple turnover, so goes the joke. (2 words)
15 This dessert is always in perfect condition.
18 Sometimes it's cubed.
21 It's often split.
22 You wouldn't make a sandwich out of it.
24 __ candy, geologist's choice.
26 You can take it.
28 Granny Smith's choice. (2 words)
29 Big animal?
31 Screamer's choice, as the saying goes. (2 words)
32 You won't get by with calling this a vegetable.

DOWN

1 You might be a sucker for one!
3 Falling citrus? (2 words)
4 Computer's munchies?
5 Square meals for dessert lovers.
8 There might be a lot of buzz about this one.
9 "Don't __--make up your mind!"
11 Holey treats.
13 __ candy, fair fare.
16 Many a dieter's downfall.
17 Baker's specialty.
19 Baked state?
20 Heavenly treat. (2 words)
23 Rhymer might enjoy coffee with it.
25 Dessert syrup.
27 Drizzled topping.
30 Nice.

35

Dan: "Did you hear what happened to that guy who stole a calendar?"
Stan: "No, what?"
Dan: "He got 12 months."

Whodunit?

Follow the clues, and you're sure to crack this case!

ACROSS

1 You might be the one.
5 Wrongdoer's helper.
6 Declaration.
9 It has to be probable.
10 Misleading fish? (2 words)
11 Falsely accuse.
12 Popular board game corner.
13 Private __, sleuth.
15 Smoking gun.
18 __ enemy #1.
19 Woo someone?
22 Wrongdoer.
25 Detective organization.
26 Wrongdoers break them.
27 It had better be a good one.
28 Detective's route.
29 Jury's judgment.

DOWN

1 Badge-wearer.
2 Squad car inhabitants.
3 "Let's find 'em."
4 Detective's black dog? (2 words)
7 English teacher's concern?
8 Lawyer's procedure.
9 "Hey, get a __!"
14 "It's the one second from the left–I'm sure of it!"
16 Prank.
17 Wrongdoer's partner.
19 Whodunit?
20 Burglar.
21 Detectives follow them.
23 Wrongdoer might be under it.
24 Print maker.

Bert was sitting in his doctor's waiting room when he heard someone shouting from the examining room, "Measles! Typhoid! Tetanus!" Perplexed, Bert went up to the receptionist and asked what was going on. "Oh, that's just Dr. Jones," she replied. "He likes to call the shots around here."

To Your Health!

You'll feel good when you finish this puzzle!

ACROSS

2 Recovery regimen.
5 "Don't swallow!"
7 "It worked for me!"
9 29 Across advice that's hard to follow.
10 Freshly minted doc.
14 Feline's look-see? (2 words)
18 Swell reducer. (2 words)
19 "One capful will do it."
20 Ham's ailment outcome?
21 Circle of docs?
22 Mop the deck with a cotton ball?
23 What ophthalmologists see.
24 It's in the dark!
28 Help in time of need.
29 He just might crown you.

DOWN

1 Bone barer. (hyph.)
2 R&R part.
3 "Take one, then call me in the morning."
4 Med grad who's made the cut?
6 It might be good or bad.
8 Bopped bone in doc's office.
11 TLC-giver.
12 Duck from this doc!
13 It's hard to be this in the waiting room!
15 Achooo! diagnosis, perhaps.
16 Pains' partners.
17 O.R. fashion statements.
19 Med clinic, in slang (hyph.), or storage of information.
24 It heals wounds.
25 Group of actors on a break?
26 Doc's organization.
27 Obnoxious one?

"Of course you're tuckered out. You know, in dog years, you're 250 years old!"

Bow-WOW!

Get a leash on this puzzle!

ACROSS

3 Warp's partner.
5 He might have one to pick with you.
6 He'll send you the test results in the morning.
8 Dog in the ring?
9 Ain't nuthin' but a (cute little) hound dog.
12 Like a dog.
15 Noted Edinburgh dog.
17 Flock watcher.
19 Every dog has one.
20 Key position of Dublin volleyball team.
22 He's yours.
23 Collar hanger. (2 words)
25 He might be one, but he won't pester you!
27 He might have a more expensive haircut than you.
28 Cavalier dog?

DOWN

1 I herd ewe.
2 They're long on love!
4 Most dogs won't quibble about it.
5 You hope it's worse than his bite.
7 Striped fellow.
10 You don't need this at the dog park.
11 "He's got it under surveillance!"
13 Scandinavian great.
14 He can bring it back.
16 27 Across need.
17 Obedience school lesson #1.
18 The best kind of dog, perhaps.
20 Dalmatian sights.
21 Can this dog fly?
24 Dog at the door, maybe.
26 Obedience school lesson #2.
27 Tented dog?

41

The most-used machine at the gym is the vending machine.

Let's Work It Out

Give your brain a stretch with this exercise!

ACROSS

3 Don't get steamed about doing this. (2 words)
4 Flexers.
6 They play the heavies in this scene.
8 You might want to take one.
12 Just roll with 'em.
13 Wear them, don't carry them.
14 Ahhh! Relief!
15 Bodybuilders' pride.
16 How many can you do, private? (hyph.)
21 Check for suitability!
24 Some do this, and that's the truth!
25 You might want to soft-pedal this one.
26 Jump to it.
28 Does this nudge your memory?
29 It will get you nowhere.
30 Exercise those lungs!

DOWN

1 Room for a gown?
2 Exerciser's destination.
5 You're all wet!
7 Trail trudge.
9 Exercise garb, for some.
10 Exercise to the max.
11 Cardio exercises.
17 It's all downhill half the time.
18 Put one foot in front of the other—quickly!
19 Exercise go-with, according to nutritionists.
20 Do Toms, Dicks, and Harrys do these, or only __?
22 Exercise path.
23 It's what bodybuilders build.
24 It's fun and games.
25 It's tu-tu much for some.
27 It's all sweat!

43

"Get your facts first, then you can distort them as you please."

Mark Twain

Fun Facts

At least that's what they claim!
How many have you heard?

ACROSS

1 You can't __ if your nose is plugged.
3 The parachute was invented 120 years before the __.
5 A duck's __ doesn't echo.
6 Women __ more than men.
8 Almonds are members of the __ family.
10 __ were originally purple, not orange.
12 __ are called "ships of the desert" because of the way they move.
14 Only female mosquitoes __.
16 The __ of an i is called a tittle.
18 An average pomegranate has more than 700 __.
19 An apple floats on __.
21 One quarter of the __ in your body are in your feet.
25 The most popular __ topping is meat, including pepperoni.
26 An ostrich can __ faster than a horse.
28 Gorillas __ up to fourteen hours per day.
30 The giant squid has the largest __ of all creatures.
31 Chewing gum while peeling onions will keep you from __.

DOWN

1 Men get __ more than women.
2 Thomas Edison, light bulb inventor, was afraid of the __.
4 First __ sent to outer space was a dog.
7 Skunks can accurately spray __ as far as ten feet.
9 Your __ beats over 100,000 times a day.
11 In the Caribbean, there are oysters that can climb __.
13 It's hard to __ with your eyes open.
15 Dolphins __ with one eye open.
17 __ are color blind when they're born.
20 Everyone's finger and __ prints are different.
22 Most of us will spend six months of our lifetime waiting at red __.
23 __ always turn left when exiting a cave is a common myth.
24 A mole can dig a __ 300 feet long in a single night.
27 You can lead a cow upstairs, but not __ is a common myth.
29 A cat has 32 muscles in each __.

44

45

**A family is a group of people
who each like a different breakfast cereal.**

Friendly Relations

Enjoy this family-friendly puzzle!

ACROSS

1 Apple pie go-with.
2 "Oh, __!"
7 Purrfect family members.
8 They're the ones with
   the stroller.
9 Chip off the old block.
10 Arf-ful family members.
13 Every family's __ has a
   few nuts.
14 The whole tribe.
15 Not an old goat.
18 Grown-up—at least in age!
20 Marital relation. (hyph.)
23 They're like family.
24 You might have one.
27 Some go deep.
29 We're linked.
30 Convent dweller.

DOWN

1 "I do!"
3 Family site.
4 So who's planning it this year?
5 Pink bedroom inhabitant.
6 Brings home the bacon.
11 It could be beef or chicken.
12 Cry if you give up.
16 The old block.
17 Yours + Mine = Family.
19 Double the fun.
21 It's new every time.
22 II
23 Relations.
25 All are good, and some
   are great!
26 She's not a picnic pest!
28 One who gets the loot?

47

A man walked into an army surplus store and asked if they had any camouflage trousers. "Yes, we have some," the clerk replied, "but we can't find them."

Dressed for the Part
Don't let this puzzle *wear* you out!

ACROSS

2 Wrap it up.

3 It's often waisted.

5 These help you rise in the world!

6 Toppers.

9 Treat with kid __.

12 Bling.

14 Dress on a slant.

16 What a voracious eater might do at the table.

17 It's not just for airplanes.

20 Changing your mind on which shoes to buy? (2 words)

23 Appendage apparel.

24 Is it big enough?

25 Tennis score.

27 Easter fashionista might wear one.

28 Yellow stinger?

DOWN

1 What the tired dog does?

2 Fashionista's delight.

4 Fashionistas are never vague about what's in it.

7 Sauna user?

8 Don't get stubborn about them.

10 Idler's preferred footwear?

11 "__ yourself!"

13 It's long.

14 "__ up your computer!"

15 Baseball follower.

18 Funds folder.

19 Like some noses.

20 First fashion? (2 words)

21 Rainbow wash. (hyph.)

22 Lettered bodice? (hyph.)

24 It might be over.

26 It's at the end of the line in fishing.

49

If it were easy, they'd call it "catching."

Let's Go Fishing!
You're sure to catch 'em all!

ACROSS

3 Fishing by __ of consciousness.
5 Grouchy one.
7 Crimson biter? (2 words)
8 How big was it?
9 Cork-and-feather float.
10 Sandwich fish.
13 Rainbow fish.
15 Wait for the weight!
16 Fisher's basket.
20 Water-whirlers. (2 words)
21 Wharf to fish from.
22 It's all in a day's fishing.
24 Rod's partner.
25 Alaskan specialty.
26 Computer virus.
27 Draggers.

DOWN

1 Site of cultivated fish?
2 Dull peepers?
4 Frozen fishing.
6 What floats yours?
7 Fish eggs.
9 Here fishy, fishy...
11 Fishing floaters.
12 Wish the fish were standing in this to take my bait!
13 This isn't football!
14 This fish is a real joiner.
17 Freshwater fishing site.
18 What the ogre is doing.
19 Fishing that's way out there. (2 words)
21 Tom Sawyer's choice.
22 Broken bone here?
23 You can hang your hat on it.

Roses Are Red...

Bluebells are blue. How many of these are known to you?

ACROSS

1 Who, me? Not!
6 They stand for thoughts, as the saying goes.
7 Christmas flower.
9 Queen Anne's fancy flower.
11 Flowers grow on them.
12 Bovine's stumble?
15 Lady's flower?
16 Cat's willow.
17 Book page?
18 East Coast school?
21 1960s flower.
24 Flower element.
26 Azure ringer?
28 Flower feature.
29 Keep quiet about this one!
30 Glorious time of day?

DOWN

2 Iris grower.
3 One by any other name...
4 Brown-eyed lass.
5 Pucker needs.
6 Popular annuals.
8 Prickly flower.
9 Purple perfumer.
10 Prickly one.
13 Spring nodder.
14 Easter flower.
19 Achoo!
20 Fresh one.
22 King of beasts in fine attire?
23 They're blue, if rhyme is true.
25 Old-fashioned lady's undergarment?
27 Is it a frond of yours?

A man sat down in a Chinese restaurant. The special for the day was Pork Rice Almond Ding, so he asked the waiter to describe the dish. "We combine pork, rice, and almonds and put the dish in the microwave." "What about the ding?" the man asked. "Oh," the waiter said, "that's the timer!"

Calling All Foodies!

Fill your plate with this culinary crossword!

ACROSS

1 It may suit you to a tee.
2 Hearty griller.
4 Man's best friend on a summer day? (2 words)
6 Top hat?
8 Zesty green.
9 Knotty snack.
11 Some hold it.
14 Achoo!
15 Citrus turf?
16 Some call it plain.
19 You can make a lot of dough with it.
22 Baker.
23 It's not hard to cook— just wing it!
24 Sandwich maker.
26 Saucy French stew.
27 Cellar dweller.

DOWN

1 Prank-loving buds?
3 It might be shredded.
5 Slice a strip.
7 Rue, rosemary, thyme, for example.
9 What's flatter than one?
10 Ladled lunch.
12 Be careful not to spill them.
13 Morning fare.
14 Italian favorite.
17 Brain food?
18 Pasta perfection. (2 words)
20 Savory dish for a chilly day.
21 Treats.
23 Fido's food.
25 It might be hard to crack.

Q: What's small, round, and blue?
A: A cranberry holding its breath.

Apples and Oranges

Let's hear it for versatile (and delicious) fruit!

ACROSS

1 It's often on a roll.
4 Fruit section.
6 Main squeeze?
8 Do they always come in twos?
9 This fruit doesn't look that bad, does it?
10 You might want to mull it over.
11 Tasty gourd.
13 Dad's favorite?
15 These fruits are a little mixed up.
18 Sour pie?
20 Look! It's going up!
22 Sassy fruit.
23 You might take a byte out of one.
26 Trembling fruit.
27 Chasms?
28 Don't strain yourself on this one!
29 Some say life's a bowl of them.

DOWN

2 Don't drop them!
3 It's part of the daily rind.
5 Sweetie's job list?
6 Fruit adept at playing a keyboard instrument?
7 Fruits that's going out tonight?
12 Drink that might be in the limelight?
13 Things are starting to gel.
14 Fruit roller.
16 Kalamata cravings.
17 They're appealing as a snack.
19 Wrathful vine hangers?
21 Artist's quiet bowl of fruit? (2 words)
24 Grizzlie's favorite?
25 It's the key to a good pie.
28 It's completely unpruned.

A GARDEN IS A THING OF BEAUTY... AND A JOB FOREVER!

True Blooms

You don't need a green thumb to enjoy this bit of gardening fun!

ACROSS

2 WWII-era garden.
3 Bump in the garden.
6 Handy garden accessories.
8 Gardener's pal.
11 Leggy apparel?
12 First garden.
13 Forest-on-a-shelf.
16 It's on the outer limits, often.
17 Don't drive here!
20 Gardener's digit.
21 Vine hanger.
22 Classy garden?
23 Fictional detective Sam.
27 Sometimes it's leggy.
29 Shapely garden.
30 He saw what was in the trunk.

DOWN

1 Nutty plot!
4 Cad in the garden?
5 Child of a bygone era.
7 Sow what?
8 Garden lights?
9 Edible garden.
10 Symbol of victory. (2 words)
14 Organic dwelling.
15 Succulent garden.
18 This garden is all over you.
19 Bloom holder.
24 Sneeze-maker.
25 Garden in mint condition?
26 It all starts here.
28 It's beneath you.
31 You might have one to hoe.

59

Two's Company...

A group of people is called a crowd, but what about groups of birds, dogs, sheep, and oxen? Follow the clues within clues for your answer!

ACROSS

4 Giggle at the __ of gargling geese!
5 Those bees are abuzz with activity.
7 One of 13 in America, or a group of ants.
8 See the laziness of those bears!
10 These birds await an airborne plane.
12 Insects are getting all over us!
14 Look and see those nightingales!
15 He compared a congregation to sheep.
17 Foxes prowl over there.
22 Kings of the jungle have a lot of self-esteem!
23 Who will steer swine across the field?
24 Are coots involved in an undercover operation?
27 Can hares help shuck corn?
29 When moles get to work, tunnels result.
30 The sparrows acted as our emcee for the event.
31 Oxen are on one side; we're on the other.

DOWN

1 Is that a package of turtles?
2 I heard the elephants!
3 Smart fish never miss class.
6 Guinea fowls are making a commotion!
9 The rabbits didn't leave a clue.
11 Those wolves are a lot of trouble.
13 Let's round up those peacocks!
16 A dog might be in one; a group of dogs is one!
18 Did you see the leopards jump high?
19 Seals and peas have something in common.
20 You don't want snakes where you sleep!
21 Pheasants in flight are like a bunch of flowers.
24 Third time is one; so it a group of finches.
25 Monkeys will march across the jungle.
26 Wasps live in one, and together, they are one.
28 Hope those toads aren't all tied up!

"Look at that speed!" said one bird to another as a jet fighter zoomed over their heads. "Hmph!" snorted the other, "You would fly that fast too if your tail were on fire!"

**Most folks are as happy
as they make up their minds to be.
Abraham Lincoln**

Feelin' Fine!

Every answer follows "Happiness is…"

ACROSS

2 Present.
4 What you hope a gadget will do.
5 Happiness out loud.
7 You can believe it.
9 It's cheesy bliss, for some.
11 Heart's happiness.
12 Second serving?
15 X marks the spot.
16 Sweet ones.
17 You might have a role in it.
21 Dictionary's offer.
22 Roof-sharers.
23 They could be online.
24 Everything's better if you get a sense of it.
26 You can opt for one.
27 Day's ray.
30 Reason for livin'.
31 It's sure to satisfy.

DOWN

1 You're at liberty to have it.
2 It's in the telling.
3 There's only one!
6 Well-being.
8 Make it a good one!
10 Cool lick. (2 words)
13 Slice of happiness?
14 It lies between too little and too much.
18 Visual happiness. (2 words)
19 Happy occasion's ring.
20 You were born with it.
25 Spa's offer.
28 Happiness to your ears.
29 Uplifting conversation.

Dad: "Son, why aren't you doing better in history? When I was your age, history was my best subject."
Son: "That's not fair. When you were my age, nothing much had happened!"

It's History!

Here are events in America's story. How will you score on these facts from the past?

ACROSS

1 People rushed for it.
5 Madison's bills.
7 1929 event.
9 Log president?
12 Ford product. (2 words)
15 1950's age.
17 Noisy 1920s.
19 Revered city?
22 9 Across birthplace.
23 New England trial town.
25 He navigated his way here.
28 Early American 13.
30 People remember it.
31 Pro Football Hall of Fame established here in 1963.
32 Redcoat's homeland.

DOWN

2 Depression-era bowl.
3 Room for NASA.
4 Tie-dyed time.
6 Washington quarters. (2 words)
8 Civil War side.
10 US and USSR chill. (2 words)
11 Early settlers' places.
13 First name in presidents.
14 Second name in presidents.
16 Native groups.
18 Last name in adages.
20 11 Down dwellers' complaints.
21 First name on the moon.
24 Famous mouse.
26 Louisiana territory state.
27 Civil War side.
29 Mark of humor.

"Son, where's your brother?"

"Well, if the ice is as thick as he says it is, he's skating. If it's as thin as I say it is, he's swimming."

Popular Pastimes

If puzzles are your favorite way to pass the time, you're in the right place! It's filled with other hobbies for you to find.

ACROSS

1 It's a purl of a pastime!
4 Don't do it in traffic!
6 You'll need keys for it.
9 You might fish for them, too.
10 You'll make a beautiful finish.
11 It's no mystery why you like these!
14 You'll have to fold, that's all.
15 Arts go-with.
18 Philatelists' focus.
19 They're usually boxed. (2 words)
22 Piece maker's pastime?
24 It might be write for you!
26 Hobby items for flighty people?
27 Canvas the place first!
30 You're into numismatics if you collect them.
32 People click with this one.

DOWN

2 Yes, there are strings attached!
3 Don't get steamed up over it!
5 You're never too old for them!
7 Pressing need for this hobby?
8 You're a gem to make it.
12 Hobbyists gaze at them.
13 It's knot for everyone.
16 "Don't needle me about it!"
17 You might have a brush with it.
20 You're going downhill fast with it!
21 Quick streak! (2 words)
23 You need a patch for it.
25 Some people take one for pleasure.
28 Geometry major's pastime?
29 Many people give a hoot for them.
31 They're heavily lettered.

Word Play

The English language is filled with words that are spelled the same (and often pronounced the same), yet have different meanings. The silly sentences provide the two clues you need to come up with the answer!

ACROSS

3 Small matter for someone under 21 years of age.

8 A gusty breeze made us get the kite string back on the spool.

9 I was drinking a citrus cooler when the car acted up—again.

10 The plane was on the tarmac when I called for a cab.

11 Drive carefully so you don't frighten the cattle.

13 Don't abandon me through that arid stretch of land!

15 I see the team leader isn't flying first-class.

16 Is there a place for a powder puff in that small car?

19 Watching a termite work is not interesting.

20 Women undergo pain when they give birth.

25 Let me go first, and I'll remove that piece of metal.

26 Whenever my dog sees tree mulch, be starts to yelp.

27 Everyone in the musical group was wearing a wedding ring.

28 The office development was an obstacle for us.

DOWN

1 He was an impartial judge at the exhibition.

2 Assembling the fireplace screen got on my nerves.

4 The archery piece was so heavy that I bent under its weight.

5 Take a look at that goose!

6 Have you ever heard a fish speak with a deep voice?

7 I promise to behave myself when I guide people.

9 He didn't fib about his rest in the hammock.

10 Will you attempt to take that case to court?

12 My dog's obedience class taught him to ride the rails with me.

14 Did the pigs scatter all that seed?

17 Get near to me, and then we'll shut the door.

18 I got up to smell the beautiful flower.

20 Are you going to carry that 2x4 when you get on the ship?

21 Let's go forward with ordering bread!

22 I was in a sticky situation when I saw the preserves.

23 He pressed us for all we know about BBQ.

24 Let's start the engine and leave that crabby man behind.

26 Clear the kitchen table! Here comes our transportation!

The difference between the right word and the almost right word is the difference between lightning and a lightning bug.
Mark Twain

More Word Play

Here's another take on word play. The clues give you one word, and then a hint to another word that is pronounced the same, but spelled differently. What's that other word?

ACROSS

2 Solo person...
   give temporarily.

5 Sums up...chopping tool.

8 Itchy parasite...take off
   running.

9 Dollars...hidden stash.

10 Appears so...stitches.

13 Orange veggie...gem's weight.

16 Coincidence...
   liturgical songs.

18 Bring up a topic...
   decorative pin.

19 Kind of tree...flock member.

21 Foundation...choir section.

23 Spiritual essence...foot part.

24 Line in London...
   helpful signal.

26 Meat on a bun...prosperous
   town merchant.

28 Rainbow's curve...
   Noah's boat.

29 Musical group...it's taboo.

DOWN

1 Made hay, so to speak...
   and pitched out water.

3 Serenity...and a part of
   the whole.

4 Perforated...and divine.

6 Pause...and scales output.

7 Log splitter...and things to do.

11 Adapt...and a church section.

12 Seashore site...and tree.

14 Hill builder...
   and uncle's wife.

15 Garden bloomer...
   and lines of them.

17 Once viewed...and a vista.

20 What we breathe...
   and a big mistake!

22 Help someone...
   and a citrus drink.

23 Vision...and a place.

24 Eerie noise at night...
   and a running stream.

25 Predator's quarry...
   and talk to God.

26 What drills do...
   and a sty critter.

27 Rule the realm...
   and precipitation.

A speech is like a wheel—
the longer the spoke, the greater the tire!

The three greatest untruths about holiday gifts are: "Easy to assemble," "Unbreakable," and "One size fits all."

Let's Celebrate!

Perhaps a few of these teaser-clues will bring back favorite holiday memories!

ACROSS

5 Hitching post?
6 Don't work too hard on this one! (2 words)
7 Service celebration. (2 words)
8 They speak on Valentine's Day. (2 words)
10 You can't bank on it.
14 June honorees.
16 Certain girls' songs.
17 February honorees.
18 You can throw your hat at it.
22 Summer sparks.
23 Park party.
28 It's jest a fun day. (2 words)
29 Season's greetings.
30 It makes bows.
31 Old Glory's glory. (2 words)

DOWN

1 Don't put them all in one basket! (2 words)
2 It's a big hit at any party.
3 You have permission to note it. (2 words)
4 You might field one.
9 One bird cries fowl!
11 Starred time.
12 Gazebo players.
13 You might have to assemble them.
15 Pre-spring springer.
19 It's golden, for some.
20 Don't rain on it!
21 Spring bouquet recipients.
24 Resolve to note it. (2 words)
25 You've got to have the dough for it.
26 It will grow on you. (2 words)
27 Sound celebration?

73

Billy was showing his playmate around his new home. "Here's my room," he said excitedly, "and here's my sister's room, and here's the nursery for the baby." Then they came to his parents' room, where he lowered his voice and said, "It's too bad, but Mom and Dad still have to share."

Home Sweet Home

No matter where you hang your hat, you'll feel at home with this puzzle!

ACROSS

3 Despite its name, you park on it.
5 Habitat.
8 Log on to this one!
10 Room with a view, maybe.
11 Despite its name, you can stand up straight on this.
13 Building blocks.
15 Room for high living?
17 Probably has crown molding.
18 Seedy space?
19 Side-by-side homes.
22 Cozy place.
25 Sometimes it's hot.
28 It's between neighbors.
29 Stalking site.
30 Impressive place.
31 Media space, maybe.

DOWN

1 Smoker.
2 Some pitch it.
4 It might roll out for you.
6 Pergola place.
7 Man's hideaway.
9 If you have this kind of home, you're really going places!
11 Story connectors.
12 It might be on top of another.
14 Saccharine site?
16 It's worn by your feet.
20 It could be front or back.
21 Slated to slant.
23 House number... or speaker's piece.
24 Rover's mobile home.
26 Fowl house.
27 It's usually more than 3 feet!

Q: What's the invention called that lets you see through the thickest of walls?
A: It's called a window.

What's New?

What do you think could have inspired these inventions?

ACROSS

1 Jelly go-with. (2 words)
3 It used to be for the birds.
4 Widest web.
6 It keeps things together.
10 It lets you know how far you've come.
11 Sound box.
13 It's a fair sight. (2 words)
16 You might be attracted to them.
17 Italian staple.
19 It has its ups and downs.
21 Frozen treat.
27 It used to be black and white.
28 Sky floaters.
29 Launchpad booster.
30 Hose.
31 What's the chance you'll get off the couch to change channels?

DOWN

1 It will help you put on a coat. (2 words)
2 It's about time!
5 You find them in closets.
7 You might woof these down! (2 words)
8 Fragrance.
9 Cheesy invention?
12 Carriage minus the horse.
14 You can have one even if you're not sitting down.
15 Finger bling. (2 words)
18 It used to be floppy.
20 Sometimes this, sometimes the hole.
22 Turf treader. (sometimes 2 words)
23 LP player. (hyph.)
24 You're write to guess this one! (2 words)
25 Hal, and others.
26 You can scale down this.

A babysitter is a teenager acting like an adult while the adults are out acting like teenagers.

Teen Trends

Feel free to get the giggles over this one!

ACROSS

2 Social, cyber and true blue.
4 Many teens have great ones.
9 Backpack fillers.
10 Find the key to this clue's answer.
11 You might trip over it, but hop to it! (2 words)
14 Formal occasion.
15 Quick snack. (2 words)
19 Partner with hopes.
21 Teens are in tune with it.
22 They can be seen almost anywhere.
24 Sweetest age.
28 Teens need an outlet for it.
29 Many teens reach for them.
30 Teen hang-ups.
31 Fish are in one, too.

DOWN

1 Come in time.
3 Left to their own, teens love them.
5 For teens, it's a slice of heaven.
6 It's sweet at any age!
7 Wee-hours must-do, maybe.
8 Memory-makers. (2 words)
12 It's where some teens learn to reed. (2 words)
13 Funds filler.
16 Everyone has one, occasionally needing adjustment.
17 Wishful winking?
18 Audible grins.
20 A bigger allowance is sure to bring them!
23 Teaming events.
26 It springs eternal.
27 Local hangout, often.

"Well, my daughter thinks I'm the worst snoop in the world. At least that's what she wrote in her diary yesterday."

Having Fun

"All work and no play…" You know the rest, so play around with these clues!

ACROSS

5 Fun go-with, especially in the snow!
8 You can do it with strollers. (3 words)
9 DIY fun.
12 Far-flung fun.
14 Sweet place to have fun.
15 It could be for thought.
16 Don't get perplexed over them!
19 If you can't be one, join 'em!
20 All you have to do is look up. (2 words)
24 It might shine in de-tail.
26 They're fun to watch.
27 You might have fun in your own.
28 Fun for you, but not your stockings.
29 Teaming fun.
30 You might be on board with them.
31 It's often staged.

DOWN

1 Iconic place of relaxation.
2 It may be sought, but never bought.
3 Joker's fun.
4 Uncommon sense?
6 You might need a coat for this.
7 Where you get a fair deal?
10 Some are cyber.
11 Park for pleasure.
13 Sideline interest.
17 Two-tired for fun?
18 You can do this solo.
21 High flyer.
22 Response to a sad face. (2 words)
23 In-tents event?
25 You might want to dip into it.

81

Sights and Sites in the City

You're sure to find your way around this urbane puzzle!

ACROSS

2 They have a point.
7 One might run through it.
9 You can bear it.
10 Diner's delights.
12 Capitol sight.
13 City fellow in raingear?
14 High living in the city.
15 It flows with the go.
16 You might stay there.
19 You can easily see through them.
20 Stop here!
22 You might follow one.
23 It stands for something.
26 Slice of the city.
28 It goes with the flow.
30 City with explosive growth? (2 words)

DOWN

1 It's a buyer's market.
2 It has lots of stories.
3 Play space.
4 It's old stuff to some.
5 Three makes one.
6 It's huge!
8 Movable merchant. (2 words)
11 Main Street site.
17 They might be elevated.
18 They're not the heavies here.
21 They don't live there.
24 It will take you to every level.
25 Honkers.
27 It's probably beneath you.
29 It might be your business.
31 It's hailed.

Q: If milk builds strong bones and healthy bodies, how come cows don't stand up straight?

Country Comforts

Drop in for a spell and make yourself at home with this puzzle!

ACROSS

1 The lowdown.
4 Fruitful plot.
7 Husky site.
11 Cool pool.
12 Milky Way?
13 Smoker.
14 Neigh-sayers.
17 You might try to get over it.
20 Mane man.
24 Works best when it's spread.
25 Just soil?
27 Outfielder.
28 Henpecked place.
30 If you're out there,
   you might be __ prime.
31 You might pine for these.
32 Here's wishing you happy ones.

DOWN

2 Main strip site.
3 Sprout site.
5 It has to do with farming.
6 Ewe see them.
8 Marshmallow roast.
9 A time of gathering on the farm.
10 You might have herd of them.
15 Angled whirls? (2 words)
16 Make hay while the sun shines.
18 Round-up site.
19 It makes the cut.
21 Chaff partner.
22 Potluck supper site.
23 They don't belong on
   your forehead!
26 Alarm on the farm.
29 Plant...or a sty critter.

Two snowmen were standing together in the Smith's front yard. One turned to the other and said, "That's funny—I smell carrots, too."

Time for a Snack!

Nibble on a few of these tasty treats!

ACROSS

3 Pigskins? (2 words)
7 Use your head for one. (2 words)
9 Sunbathing grapes?
12 Dad's bad joke?
13 Top these chips, if you can!
15 "Dad, you want one?"
16 What many snacks aren't.
17 This could give you a tug.
19 Snack sack.
22 Shivering cow? (2 words)
23 Tango alternative?
27 You pick it up in a carton.
28 Who made the apple go in circles? (2 words)
30 Polly's favorite snacks.
31 Knot food.
32 Spiced bites.

DOWN

1 Beach-goer might take one.
2 Digital snack?(2 words)
4 It's often roasted.
5 Campfire sandwich.
6 Deli choice.
8 Rings to make you cry?
10 English tea treats.
11 It's often wrapped.
14 It might string you along.
18 What Hansel and Gretel needed. (2 words)
20 It's a nutty snack.
21 Breakable peanut.
24 It's often roped.
25 Colorful tidbits.
26 Break fluid?
29 Bear with this one.

87

"Mommy!" Carrie cried as she rushed into the house. "Zach broke my new baby doll!" "Oh, I'm sorry, sweetheart" her mother replied. "When did this happen?" "The minute I hit him over the head with it."

Just Kidding!

Let your inner child play with this one!

ACROSS

1 There's a key to it. (2 words)
4 Disappearing act? (3 words)
5 You might get pushed on them.
10 It has its ups and downs. (hyph.)
11 It's hard to get past them!
12 Shelf-styled trains, boats and planes.
16 Become your alter ego! (hyph.)
17 Warren you wander in.
20 They could buy online.
22 Rainforest bars? (2 words)
24 Street surfer?
26 You might have a jingle with it. (2 words)
27 They have cells. (2 words)
29 Puzzle that puts you in pieces!
30 Little one's little one. (2 words)
31 Sometimes there's a price on it.
32 You have all of yours, for sure!

DOWN

2 Think "five, six" for this answer. (3 words)
3 It needs evenly matched sides.
6 You just have to roll with them.
7 Island ring. (2 words)
8 Not jills.
9 Plush hug. (2 words)
13 Opening for a toothed fastener? (2 words)
14 Lofty place to play.
15 It's a send-up.
18 Pole jumper. (2 words)
19 Downhill ride.
21 You'll get to circulate. (3 words)
23 It's a pail place.
25 It'll come back to you.
28 Give these a spin!

A young woman and her boyfriend had been dating for quite a while, and she was eager to start talking about marriage. Nothing happened, however, after still more time together. Then one evening the two went to a Chinese restaurant. Scanning the menu, the boyfriend casually asked her, "So, how do you like your rice? Steamed or fried?" She looked at him and said, "Thrown."

Marvelous Milestones

When you find the answers to this one, there's another milestone you've reached!

ACROSS

2 Soldiers level with it.
5 Dutiful do.
6 It's permanent.
10 You did it!
11 You get credit for it.
14 It's just a phase.
16 Crossroads, maybe. (2 words)
18 Some say it starts at 40.
21 It may bring you a windfall.
22 You take them one at a time.
25 You might cruise through it.
28 Primary employment. (2 words)
29 Life-altaring event?
30 Wet event?
31 You might cap it.
32 It might be golden.

DOWN

1 It's elementary. (2 words)
3 You remember the first one.
4 It takes you to the next level.
7 It could be a starter.
8 Reach for them!
9 It's fully satisfactory.
12 Resolve to start now. (3 words)
13 Fix a wheel?
15 It's a matter of degree.
17 It has class from the past!
19 Majority number. (hyph.)
20 You might mind yours.
23 It's what you talk about.
24 Heartfelt activity. (3 words)
26 Changing times. (2 words)
27 Age gauge.

A manager, looking over the log kept by his IT staff, noticed that several entries listed the problem as PICNIC. He asked one of the technicians what it meant. The technician replied with a grin: "Problem In Chair, Not In Computer."

Life's a Picnic!

Grab a basket, sandwiches, and soda, and you're ready for a picnic…but a pencil is all you need for a puzzle!

ACROSS

4 They're often corny.
5 Don't let it sour you.
7 German citizen?
9 Hot condiment.
10 Sprayed shade.
12 You might commune with it.
16 Seeded slice.
18 Squeezed tomatoes.
19 Hot letters.
20 It has legs.
21 You shouldn't need to cut it.
23 Tresses pin up or Patty's put on.
24 Stopping place.
26 You can jump in it.
28 Gritty ground.
30 Turf presider? (2 words)
31 Dieter's delight. (2 words)

DOWN

1 Chilling site. (2 words)
2 You might swing over there.
3 Picnic blazer.
6 Picnic packer.
8 Bird-mandible watchers?
11 Hand-held meal.
13 Picnic pall. (2 words)
14 Don't get in one!
15 Tossed tubers. (2 words)
17 You can spread it.
22 Shades of picnics.
25 Diamond event.
27 You'll get plenty of waves there.
29 Picnic season.
32 Picnic pests.

Tell a man there are three hundred billion stars in the universe, and he believes you. Tell him a bench has wet paint on it, and he has to touch it to make sure.

Mother Nature

Enjoy the great outdoors with this puzzle!

ACROSS

6 Big drop of H_2O?
9 It will grow up.
11 Outdoor atmosphere. (2 words)
12 They go with the flow.
13 Canine's favorite time! (2 words)
14 Some people have doors for them.
16 This one's easy!
17 It could be dated.
19 Original beamer.
22 One might have his head in one.
24 Coulds and shoulds partners?
25 You can get to the bottom of it.
26 It waves at you.
27 This will come to you.
28 It's all over.

DOWN

1 They're relieved in the spring.
2 Wax go-with.
3 Sunset hour.
4 Hustles and bustles.
5 Everyone talks about it.
7 They might be rolling.
8 Cyber-snips?
10 Little house site.
15 Spring at this one!
16 Sad orb? (2 words)
17 Face creams, maybe.
18 They looked peaked.
20 What the cook does to the cast-iron pan?
21 Say "crepuscule," and impress your friends!
23 Don't stumble over this one.
27 It's the real lowdown.

Next year we're going to spend vacation somewhere near our budget.

Take a Break

We all need a vacation now and then, but not from fun puzzles!

ACROSS

3 Vacation manager.
(2 words)
5 No man is one, they say.
6 It may decide how far you can go.
9 This one's a floater.
11 Selfie, maybe.
12 Vacation span, for many.
(2 words)
13 Vacation glossies.
16 Routers.
17 Far-afield field trip.
18 It's packed.
19 Shuffle again?
20 LAX and others.
24 It might come with a view.
(2 words)
26 Lounge chair invitation.
28 Shades of sunshine.
29 Pond-hopping destination.

DOWN

1 You'll have to pitch it.
2 Coast on over!
3 It might take you for a ride.
(2 words)
4 Your pass to pleasure.
6 You might sail in one.
7 Blast-from-the-past sites.
8 Vacation greetings.
10 Vacation high points are here!
13 What's often broken during vacation.
14 Powder sliders.
15 Remember when.
21 You might have a lap there.
22 Mileage saver, maybe.
23 You'll find sweaters there.
25 Vacation dampener.
27 This vacation site has depth.

A good laugh is like
manure to a farmer.
It doesn't do any good
until you spread it around.

Too Funny!

You might find yourself laughing at this puzzle!

ACROSS

2 Jollity.
3 Unkempt canine's tail?
  (2 words)
6 Non-rational joke?
8 They're jest like us!
9 Owl funny was it, anyway?
10 Field humor?
15 It's at your elbow. (2 words)
16 Animated humor.
18 They're contagious!
20 Tragedy's partner.
21 You get a sense of it.
23 Anecdotally,
   Queen Victoria wasn't.
25 There was once a witty rhyme...
26 Queue at the beverage table?
   (2 words)
27 Rap-a-Tap joke? (2 words)

DOWN

1 Fun for the birds?
2 Handy speakers?
3 Worn humor.
4 High school club.
5 Seasonal laughter. (3 words)
7 They're all for show.
11 Purler's tale?
12 Burst of humor.
13 Clipped quip. (hyph.)
14 Soundless laugh.
17 Laughable pratfall.
19 Groaners.
20 Laugh in low gear?
22 Picture strip.
24 Rising laughter?
26 Laughable language.

One astronaut asks another astronaut if he has ever heard of the planet Saturn. He replies, "I'm not sure, but it has a familiar ring."

Look Up!

Scan the skies for these answers!

ACROSS

3 Don't get pulled into it.
(2 words)
6 They're depressed.
7 Northerner's navigational light.
8 What goes around,
comes around.
9 America's space place.
13 Billions and billions of stars!
14 Eye to the sky.
16 Halley's scrubber?
17 All-star picture.
21 Excellent!
24 Path to the dairy? (2 words)
25 It has a ring to it.
26 Chocolate planet?
27 Short wave? (2 words)
28 Sparkly spinner, a neutron star.
30 Recently redefined planet.

DOWN

1 Universal harmony.
2 Invisible lunar phase. (2 words)
4 Heavenly.
5 Small scoop of stars. (2 words)
10 Mega-star explosion.
11 A cluster of these makes
a shower.
12 Largest planet.
13 The apple proved it.
15 Angelic topper.
18 Solar dots.
19 What you might do with
a cradle?
20 Outer limit's radio waver.
22 Light bands in the sky.
23 Astronomically long. (2 words)
25 Let's get earnest about this!
29 Roswell lander.

You know things aren't going well for yourself when you walk out of a memory-improvement class and can't remember where you parked your car.

Selfie

That's right—it *is* all about you! All answers follow "self"!

ACROSS

6 You might put yourself under it.
7 Too much of it goes before the fall.
11 Your thoughtful approval of you.
13 "Hey, here I am!"
14 Soundly adjusted.
15 You might nurse it.
18 Backward pat.
19 Egoist's expertise.
21 Be the king (or queen) of your castle?
24 You are all you need.
27 Approval!
28 Personal issue?
29 "Awww, poor me!"
30 Your potential.
31 You learned it all by yourself.

DOWN

1 You can't put a price on it.
2 It was at your own speed.
3 Figure yourself out!
4 You're this if you can think for yourself.
5 DIY.
8 Personal martial arts?
9 You don't need a doctor to do it.
10 "I will do this!"
12 Selfie.
16 "Can't I do anything right?"
17 You're the boss.
20 "I have a heart for me!"
22 Prophecy you make come true.
23 Aretha Franklin spelled it out for you.
25 DIYer's reading preference.
26 You walk away from it.

103

The worst part of paying $200 for a babysitter to watch the kids for an evening is returning home and finding that she had a better time than you did.

Oh, Baby!

Don't let the clues in this puzzle *rattle* you!

ACROSS

2 It's changeable.
4 Feeder.
5 Snowy sheets.
8 They're plush!
10 Room's reflection.
11 First word, maybe.
13 Room shiner.
15 Tiara tot.
17 They're often in the pink.
19 You'll find a leaf in it.
20 They'll lie.
24 Contentment-maker.
25 The first are usually shaky.
28 You might hang on them.
29 You might be well-versed in it.

DOWN

1 You might spread it.
2 Baby's drawers.
3 You might go back and forth on this one.
6 They'll drop down.
7 It has bounce to it.
9 Cozy coos.
12 Art on the wall.
14 Cuddle cubs. (2 words)
16 Don't cheat on this one!
18 It keeps moving.
21 Ear-to-ear statements.
22 Growing room?
23 The eyes he has for you.
26 Seating room.
27 You have them–they're just more expensive!

**Money talks...
but all mine ever says is
"good-bye".**

Dollars and Sense

Hope this puzzle about money matters makes *sense* to you!

ACROSS

3 Money keeper.
5 Sow money? (2 words)
9 Golden-touch man.
12 Lira replacer.
13 Weighty money in London.
14 British standard.
16 Ruddy penny. (2 words)
18 Purrfect fund?
19 Some pan it.
22 Minor money? (2 words)
23 You might watch them run.
25 Money flyer?
26 Hard disk?
27 You knead it!
28 Mint print.

DOWN

1 Money laid aside? (2 words)
2 Paper wait?
4 Atomic 28.
5 Fund place.
6 With this and a leg, you can buy.
7 Money-mad one.
8 Bullion bank. (2 words)
10 Infusion.
11 It's often small.
15 Money for your salad days?
17 It might stretch beyond
 your money.
20 It's thin.
21 Wad of bills.
23 Food for your wallet.
24 It's on the barrelhead.

Before takeoff, the flight attendant announced to all passengers: "If anyone would like some gum before we start, it will prevent your ears from popping as we gain altitude." After the flight landed, everyone got off, except one man. "Do you need some assistance?" the attendant inquired. "Speak up, please," the man yelled, "I can't hear you with all this gum in my ears!"

Places to Go!

Here are some sites to sightsee on your next trip away from home!

ACROSS

2 You might *barge* down it.
4 Arizona's *big chasm.*
   (2 words)
7 *George's* place?
8 There's great food to *gobble!*
10 You can *fry* with it!
11 You might walk its *broad way.*
   (2 words)
12 A visit there will *spice* up your life.
13 Is *rain* always on the *plain?*
16 Will the *wind mill* around us there?
18 *Ach,* let's go!
20 It provides a *peak* experience.
22 Are you *roamin'* around there?
25 *Ipanema* girl's home.
27 You'll have a *lulu* of a time there!
29 I *Prado* will go there soon.
30 It's all *Greek* to me!
31 Let's *cruise* over it.

DOWN

1 *Can ya'* go on a safari with me?
3 *Cold pole?*
5 *Fjord* drivers are welcome.
6 Let's *waltz* on over.
9 USA *amigo's* nation.
13 Does it *needle* you to visit this city?
14 *Oui* might go there someday.
15 *Rhymer's* delight.
   (2 words)
17 *Mummy,* please come, too!
19 It's been *green* forever!
21 Are you *loched* into going?
23 You might *rush in* there!
24 You could find an *Inuit inn.*
26 It's *tea* place to go!
28 What do people there call their *good dishes?*

108

Winter is the time of year when people start going to places where they can pay two-hundred dollars a day to experience the same heat that they were complaining about all summer long!

Brrrr!

Warm up with this puzzle all about winter!

ACROSS

2 Controlled burn.
4 A romantic place for you and your flame.
9 Where you'll find the latest scoop?
12 Car part.
15 Cold cuts? (2 words)
16 Bright spots.
19 Not a baaad wrap!
21 Icy fella?
23 It might be patchy.
24 You could be below it.
25 Marshmallow go-with. (2 words)
27 Biting weather descriptor.
28 Sloping pastime.
30 Deciduous tree descriptor.
31 They're handy in the winter.
32 It's not clear to anyone.

DOWN

1 You might make this sport a goal.
3 Stand-offish stare?
5 Winter hangers.
6 Fall-back time for cool-down days.
7 They wander in the wind.
8 Fuzzy white kitty's moniker.
10 Personal portable rain roof.
11 Winter angler. (2 words)
13 They're not the cat's pajamas.
14 You might yearn to see one.
17 It could sleigh you!
18 Windbag's weather report!
20 That's thaw, folks!
22 It's a blast in some places!
26 Season's seasoning.
29 You can see it in the cold.

111

A tourist admired a necklace worn by a local tribesman. "What's it made of?" she asked. "Alligator teeth," he replied. "I imagine it means as much to you as a string of pearls would mean to me," she said. "Not really," the tribesman countered. "Anyone can open an oyster."

Bring Out the Bling!

Here's a gem of a puzzle for you!

ACROSS

5 It could play a short role in your life.
6 Carat cradle.
9 You'll be tickled to wear one!
10 Geometric jewelry style. (2 words)
13 Worn by the light of the moon?
14 It's not real!
16 Isle gem.
18 Reef find.
21 Lobe probe.
22 It makes a good impression.
23 It's just for frills.
24 Tress dress.
25 You might string them along.
27 A good one is well-connected.
28 Some people are as good as that!
29 Snaky statement.

DOWN

1 Don't get unhinged over one!
2 It's got you surrounded.
3 Foot wrap.
4 You might find the time for one.
5 Some things are clear as that!
6 It opens doors for you.
7 Beaded bangle.
8 Rubber wrapper with a cause.
11 Hot coal.
12 You wear them on your sleeve. (2 words)
15 Sparkler in suspense.
17 It shines.
18 Hold on tight!
19 Bitty bauble at the cinema?
20 Olympians aim to wear one.
26 You've got to give them a hand.

How Come

- There's mileage, yardage, and footage... but no inchage?
- We say "after dark" when what we mean is "after light?"
- Bleachers are called "stands" when they're meant for sitting down?

Listen!

What made that noise? The italicized words are clue boosters!

ACROSS

5 It *sizzled* at the picnic.

6 Their *clatter* at dinnertime was deafening.

7 The *tweet* things were all *aflutter*.

10 I lost track of its *clickety-clack*.

11 I heard a *crunch* when I hit the dip. (2 words)

13 She was having a *purrfect* day.

14 He was *ribbeted* to the lily pad.

17 I couldn't get the *jingle* out of my head.

20 Who's the *ding-a-ling* on the porch?

21 She thought it was a *big giggle*.

22 Some folks say it's a *mooving* sound.

25 Is there enough *vroom* here?

26 I heard a *click* as I worked at my computer.

27 We'll be *dressed* in a *snap*.

28 She did *flips*, but they ended in *flops*.

DOWN

1 It was a real *hum*dinger of a tune!

2 The sound of those *creaks* goes *up and down*.

3 The breeze makes a *whirled* of difference.

4 The *thump* was met with *whoops* of cheering.

8 It *fizzled* out on us.

9 I *quacked* up when I heard the joke!

11 Hey, who *squealed* on us?

12 It *stormed* in the *boom* town.

15 I *warmed* to the *crackle* quickly.

16 Don't get *ticked* off when you hear it!

17 Have you heard the latest *buzz*?

18 They're part of ancient *hissstory*.

19 He's *barking* up the wrong tree.

23 It *splat* just like that!

24 We were having a *roaring* good time at the zoo!

A teacher spread out a world map in front of her class. "Tommy," she said, "please come to the map and find America." Dutifully Tommy approached the map and put his hand on the correct country. "Very good!" the teacher beamed as Tommy returned to his seat. "Now class," she said, "who discovered America?" Lisa's hand shot up. "Tommy!" she shouted.

In the USA

See how many of these *state*ments you can figure out!

ACROSS

1 When *Helena* fell in a hole, she pined for *Jackson*.

4 He *raleighed* us with his *cardinal* cry. (2 words)

5 Didn't he *first state* that he knew?

9 The *twins* will visit the *cities*.

10 *Dodge* this *city?* Certainly not!

11 *Saguaro* stuck here?

13 The *bluebird* of happiness took her out of her *misery*.

16 *Sunny, orange* you planning to visit?

18 You might listen to a *little rock* 'n roll.

19 *Providence* willing, I'll visit you. (2 words)

21 It's a *boise* place.

23 In *August*, we'll say *ta*-ta.

28 She's just *peachy* proud to be there!

29 Did *Lincoln* ever sleep here?

30 Keep a *hawk-eye* out for his *corny* pranks.

DOWN

2 *Juneau* this one, for sure!

3 Autumn made the *lan'* sing.

4 *Violet* hoed her *garden*, then *trent on* her way. (2 words)

6 *Baton* down the *rouge*, would you?

7 I took a *mountain* of luggage on a *rocky* road.

8 *Ho-no*, it's a *lulu* of a place!

12 Why was he *mad* at *his son?*

14 He *salt*ed the *lake* with bait.

15 *Eureka!* Now I've won the *gold!*

17 The fighters hoped to reach *concord*. (2 words)

20 *Who's 'ere* who lives there?

22 *Shy Ann* didn't say anything.

24 He sat like a *statue* until given *liberty* to go. (2 words)

25 *Carson*, why can't I wear *silver?*

26 *Say, Lem*, are you coming?

27 *Austin*, are you joining us?

A man was wheeling himself frantically down the hospital hall just before his operation. Stopping him, the nurse asked, "What's the matter?" "They were getting me ready for surgery, and I heard the nurse say, 'Now it's a very simple operation, so don't worry. It will be all right.'" The nurse replied, "She was trying to comfort you. What's so scary about that?" "She was talking to the surgeon!"

All In a Day's Work

Don't *labor* over these punny phrases about occupations.

ACROSS

4 Problems for the farmer kept __ up.

6 The masseuse __ his clients the wrong way.

7 The historian found no __ in his job.

9 The plumber's business went down the __.

11 Balloonists feared high __.

13 The overworked chef had too much on her __.

14 The clockmaker hired a __ hand.

15 The dartboard maker __ too high.

18 The barista tired of the daily __.

19 The door maker looked for another __.

21 The surgeon quit because his __ wasn't in it.

24 The photographer's business stopped __.

25 Soon the steel worker lost his __.

26 The new airline couldn't get off the __.

28 He couldn't __ at the orange juice factory.

DOWN

1 Paving cul-de-sacs is a __ job. (hyph.)

2 The railroad worker was __.

3 The baker was fired for too much __.

5 She worked in banking until she lost __.

6 The hotdog vendor worked with __.

8 The prospector's job was thoroughly __.

10 The archaeologist found his business in __.

12 He quit making lawn chairs when the business __.

13 The senior numbers theorist was past his __.

16 The computer rep lost his __.

17 The __ agent quit because her business was going nowhere.

20 The origami artist got tired of all the __.

22 The tailor was hanging on by a __.

23 The banana grower's business started __.

27 The plower soon found himself in a __.

118

> We are all here for a spell;
> get all the good laughs you can.
> Will Rogers

What's So Punny?

Your clues are puns, riddles, grins...ok, and maybe a few groaners.

ACROSS

1 Its tunes are long drawn out.
3 It gets more sheepish with age.
5 It's the one thing that's permanent.
10 It's easier given than taken.
11 Nap sack.
13 One is in knot, but not in not.
15 Look out, it's glass!
16 Sage-saga on TV.
18 You feel it when you don't.
22 It usually has a house attached.
25 Little stinkers? (2 words)
28 It's all keyed up.
29 It prevents baldness.
30 They lie all the time.
31 He's always me-deep in
\conversation.

DOWN

2 He says he's a paragrapher.
4 It's not what it's cracked up to be.
6 Hard-learned education.
7 You might use it in a pinch.
8 Night light.
9 You'll find them boring.
12 Sick bird?
14 She turns flops into successes.
17 The difference between here and there.
19 One makes light of everything.
20 Piece makers.
21 Altared friendship?
23 It often starts with a start.
24 Giraffe among birds.
26 Pool room.
27 Faith lift.

Diner: "Waiter, is there any soup on the menu?"
Waiter: "There was, sir,
but I wiped it off."

It's on the Menu

Choose your answers from these mouth-watering clues!

ACROSS

1 Fancy these pancakes!
6 "Oh, shucks!"
7 All eyes are on them.
9 Chef, don't get out of shape when it's this!
10 Some chefs get puffed up over these.
12 It's served on a stick.
14 Don't let this menu choice mix you up.
17 Dough you want some?
21 Pasta pleasure, cooked just enough. (2 words)
22 Sweet endings.
25 It's served with gusto.
26 Your server might toss it.
28 There's something fishy here.
29 It's eggstra good.
30 Dippy chickpeas.
31 No bones about it, you'll like it!

DOWN

1 Spice of life for Louisianans!
2 Light shower.
3 Some people have a confused look about this.
4 Served at a banquet, with sarcasm on the side.
5 Of course course you like it!
8 Look at these choices from all angles.
11 Entrée here! (2 words)
13 It makes a homerun cake!
15 It's in a sauce fit for royalty. (3 words)
16 This will bring it home. (2 words)
18 Clearly a wonderful soup.
19 Simple turn for an egg. (2 words)
20 'Specially sad dish? (2 words)
23 You can have one in short order.
24 Appetizing finger food.
27 Word that can signal "expensive."

123

While eating at a pricey steakhouse, a man asked the waiter to please pack the leftovers for their dog. "Whoopee!" his son exclaimed excitedly, "we're going to get a dog!"

Let's Eat Out!

Got an appetite? Maybe these eateries and "eating" words will give you some ideas!

ACROSS

1 Troop in for dinner. (2 words)
4 Workplace break place.
6 What a spread!
7 Servers. (2 words)
8 Green eatery. (2 words)
11 Corner coffee stop, maybe.
12 Eatery along the way.
14 Fly in for a special! (hyph.)
16 London afternoon sipping stop.
22 Open air eatery.
25 Pick what you want here.
26 On-the-road eatery. (2 words)
27 Command to a Chinese dog? (2 words)
28 Food lovers' festive feast.

DOWN

2 Island poi party.
3 Speedy delivery? (2 words)
5 Nutritionist's choice. (2 words)
6 Casual cozy meet-up spot.
9 Where some things rise, but diets fall.
10 "Rye are we going here?"
13 Retro restaurant.
15 Sack a sandwich.
17 Meating place?
18 Hot place to grill.
19 Cowboy's canteen. (2 words)
20 Carton cuisine for dining in.
21 Single seating at 13 down.
23 Soda seller's site.
24 Eat in the cars with the stars. (hyph.)

A lie gets halfway around
the world before the truth has a
chance to get its pants on.
Winston Churchill

Things to Think About

Reflect on these clues, and you might feel inspired!

ACROSS

2 Last word in prayer.
6 Faith and love's partner.
7 Look favorably upon...
8 Holy handiwork.
11 Shining guideline. (2 words)
13 Resplendent.
19 Heaven on earth.
21 Position yourself all over again?
22 Walk on the straight and
   narrow one.
23 Rejuvenation.
24 You simply can't explain it.
26 Pizza guy's job?
27 There's lots of it!
28 The whole thing is in
   His hands.
30 How angels greet each other?

DOWN

1 Awe-filled.
3 Heart of hearts.
4 You might feel its beat.
5 "He will be called...
   Prince of __."
9 Reliance on God.
10 Seeker's search.
11 November holiday's theme.
12 Sacred question; the divine
   unknown.
14 Messengers of God.
15 Moves you to feel or do
   something meaningful.
16 Repentant one's desire.
17 TLC grows from it.
18 66 sacred books.
20 The Word is __.
25 Sunday service center.
29 He's above it all.

127

"Dad, I think I flunked my science test today."

"Now, son, don't be so negative."

"Okay, Dad. I'm positive I flunked my science test today."

School Daze

You're sure to score well on this test!

ACROSS

3 Examine your soda can? (2 words)
6 Honor roll. (2 words)
8 Ancient scribe's laptop?
9 Test watcher.
12 Fresh cadet.
16 School day's starting place.
18 It's a steep climb for some.
20 Students wouldn't swap this school!
22 Students are attracted to this school.
24 Every student's favorite.
26 On-the-road learning experience. (2 words)
27 Direction a class is taking?
28 Sherlock's favorite school?
29 Teachers don't have to be sophisticated to have this.
30 Subjects' swan songs.

DOWN

1 AWOL!
2 Grads that have "been there".
4 A school to study astronomy?
5 It's the school's swinging place.
7 It's a paper, and a semester.
10 Head-stuffing session?
11 Hot time to attend this school!
13 Administrative panel.
14 Former stylus.
15 A way with language.
17 When you go to this door, your knees might do the knocking.
19 Basics.
21 They're well-schooled in school.
23 Growing place for little sprouts?
25 Some people learn them the hard way!

129

A man, attending his first car racing event at the speedway, watched for several minutes, then turned to his friend and remarked: "Seems to me if they started earlier, they wouldn't have to drive so fast."

Sporting Fun

Get your game on and tackle these clues!

ACROSS

4 You'll have to jump over them.
7 It's repeatedly bowled over.
9 It's one way to get a wave.
11 It goes full circle.
12 Winner's win.
14 Pass it forward!
16 The puck's on ice.
17 It's sharp to win them.
20 They're really deep sometimes.
22 She'll flip over you!
23 It's in the running.
25 Shirt on the green?
26 Some jump through them.
28 You might take a stab at it.
29 Net lob.

DOWN

1 Dawdle around?
2 Game group.
3 Stands for seats.
5 Pressing rod?
6 They could be parallel.
8 It has its drawbacks.
10 He calls 'em as he sees 'em.
13 Fisher's gear.
15 These players horse around.
18 Love means nothing when you play.
19 They light up the courts.
20 Fifty percent of skiing.
21 Use your head in this one.
24 Reached-for post.
27 Green standard.

Remember Moses started out as a basket case too, and God made something of him anyway.

Beloved Bible Stories

These Bible people and places are dear to the hearts of many!

ACROSS

2 His name means "Rock."
3 He parted water.
4 Ten plagues sufferer.
6 Awe-filled experience!
10 Where 3 Across was hidden.
13 Old Testament wise guy.
14 "Prodigal Son," for example.
17 Major missionary.
20 New Testament letter.
21 First man.
23 Israel's second king.
25 Israelites' twelve.
27 Beatitudes word.
28 Psalm 23 topic.
29 Follower.
30 Calvary sight.

DOWN

1 Last Supper site. (2 words)
3 Nativity visitors.
5 Noah's arc?
7 Ten plagues place.
8 Savior.
9 Beginning garden.
10 8 Down's childhood home.
11 Multi-colored coat wearer.
12 Isaiah, for example.
15 Where He walked.
16 Guiding light for 3 Down.
18 "Teach us to pray" prayer.
19 A giant fight.
22 "Magnificat" speaker.
24 First book.
26 Jonah swallower. (2 words)

As the animals were boarding the ark, Noah turned to his wife and said, "Now I've herd everything!"

It's a Zoo Out There!

Tour the menagerie with these clues!

ACROSS

4 He goes from one spot to the other.
7 Has he ever heard a discouraging word?
10 He sees everything in black and white.
11 Can you get them on the scales?
12 Mimic this one!
13 Australian cuddler.
14 This seabird is out of breath!
15 Will he ever come out of his shell?
17 He thinks it's funny.
18 "Charmed to meet you!"
19 They're in the fold.
21 "That one is really hamming it up for us!"
22 Bars, wrench, or this critter!
24 This critter is always changing!

DOWN

1 Maybe you don't give a hoot about them.
2 Is he telling the truth?
3 What he eats goes a long ways.
5 Distinctive African equid.
6 There's a trumpet in his trunk.
7 They like to hang around.
8 Healthy critter full of ant-i-bodies?
9 Chill seeker. (2 words)
12 "Sure, but can he subtract?"
13 He's never out of bounds.
14 You believed his colorful tail?
16 Tabby's big cousin.
20 Has this bird gone crackers?
23 Antlered one.

135

> Poetry is the rhythmical
> creation of beauty in words.
>
> Edgar Allan Poe

Rhyme Time

In this puzzle, each answer is made up of two rhyming words.

Here's an example: Clue – Hilarious hare. Answer – Funnybunny

ACROSS

1 Sleep like a log.
4 Norseman on a motorcycle.
9 Bovine fight.
10 Happy sheepdog.
12 Monotonous tile design.
14 Trojan horse.
15 Less effective orator.
16 Footwear wrecker.
18 Nicer sauna-sitter.
21 Calm argument.
25 Love-struck feline.
26 Wrinkly clergyman.
27 Pal who fell in a puddle.
29 Bee's dance.
30 Snake's dance.

DOWN

2 Dance for a tropical fruit.
3 Stoat's painting stand.
5 One who lives in the basement.
6 Cheese on a toboggan.
7 Serious news article.
8 Stylishly sophisticated pachyderm.
11 Frosted two-wheeler.
13 Choristers' robes.
17 Cruise ship's restaurant.
19 Defiant little rock.
20 High temperature of a dam-building rodent.
22 Dark musher.
23 Comedic cat.
24 Relaxed stringed instrument.
28 Platter spinner's nightwear.

> Poetry: The best words
> in the best order.
>
> Samuel Taylor Coleridge

More Rhyme Time

Keep your rhyming-timing going!

ACROSS

1 Well-made head covering.
3 Frightening songbird.
6 Aggressive sheep.
9 Shipbuilder's remaining pole.
11 Sassy flower child.
13 Light brown twine.
17 Break-time treat shelf.
19 Dive in the pool.
20 Roll just out of the oven.
24 Energetic dog, cheerier than another
26 Pooch in the rain.
27 Train-hopping wind instrument.
28 Laughter in a convent.
29 Chilly Christmas.
30 Stinging insects' snow-sliders.

DOWN

2 Yellow fruit from Cuba.
4 Woven-reed headrest.
5 Zealous maid.
7 Play about a camel's cousins.
8 Scandinavian's aches.
10 Fairly angry root veggie.
12 Shrimp's cousin's strength.
14 Lawyer-trained droopy-eared hound.
15 Charge to use the golf course.
16 Danger in an Italian canal city.
18 Captain of a sailing vessel.
21 Red sled.
22 Language of a wild Australian dog.
23 Satisfactory climbing plant.
25 Timepiece on a pier.

Did you hear about the two dogs that went to a flea circus? All the performers went home with them.

It's an Old-Time Circus!

Ladies and gentlemen, children of all ages, step right up and give this a try!

ACROSS

1 He goes around in circles.
6 Canvas the scene where this stands! (2 words)
8 It's a moving spectacle!
9 One hump or two?
10 It makes a good catch.
13 Wagon team.
14 Circus brothers.
16 He might flip over you!
18 Circus man P.T.
21 Performers take a swing at it.
24 They're jest having fun!
25 It could be higher than a stovepipe. (2 words)
26 It might be the biggest one on Earth.
27 He has a tall order to fill. (2 words)
29 It's chips off the old block.

DOWN

2 They haul trunks.
3 "Come one, come all!" caller.
4 Performer's bling.
5 Silent partner?
7 Circus ad.
11 Piped-in music?
12 Fan's purchase.
15 Wearable dazzlers.
17 Knotty performer?
19 Circus big wheel.
20 He always gets ahead. (2 words)
21 It's a thin line for performers.
22 They have a ball multi-tasking.
23 Performer might shoot right out of one!
28 Wide-eyed watchers.

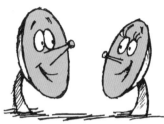

Two satellite dishes met on a rooftop, fell in love, and got married. The ceremony wasn't much, but the reception was wonderful.

On with the Show!

This puzzle is for your viewing—and doing—pleasure!

ACROSS

1 It's the spice of life.
3 Some are fielded.
5 Not live.
7 They show both sides.
10 It goes before action.
12 Laugh track's need.
15 Some are spots.
17 They might go solo.
18 Girls, don't brood over it! (2 words)
19 TV stage.
21 Clean aria? (2 words)
22 It's a sound concept.
25 Rough outlines.
27 You might play along. (2 words)
29 Biopic, for one.
30 They take their cues from it.

DOWN

2 Q&A session.
4 They don't always keep their cool.
6 Animated experiences.
8 There's a first time for everything.
9 Sofa-sitters, often.
11 "Anyone out there?"
12 Show shiner.
13 They'll manage.
14 Godzilla is in one. (2 words)
16 Impromptu action, it's said. (2 words)
20 This show might put you to sleep. (2 words)
23 Cosmetic application.
24 Some stand up for it.
26 This job sounds like two letters of the alphabet.
28 It's what's happening.

Husband: "Honey, if we decided to move to someplace in Alaska where we could live in a cabin without electricity and I could hunt for our food, what would you miss most?"

Wife: "You."

Place Chase

Each clue contains a word (or words) that is a rhyme or near rhyme with the answer word, a place name. Let's go!

ACROSS

2 Asian house.
4 Island tuba.
6 Men were in Colorado.
8 Asian long song. (2 words)
11 Asian myna.
12 African dad.
14 Central American police.
16 British tales.
17 Park fellow's phone.
18 Near-eastern warden.
19 Lost in Massachusetts.
21 Her line in California.
24 Home in Italy.
26 European dance.
29 Sell corn in Australia.

DOWN

1 Rain o' Texas.
3 Georgia bacon.
5 So low in Africa.
7 Greek toads.
9 More hay in Scandinavia.
10 Montana patient's fillings.
13 Texas palace.
15 Scandinavian wren park.
18 To know Alaska.
20 The fall in Asia.
22 Aegean treat.
23 Northeastern tape wad. (2 words)
25 New England train.
27 Notre Dame terrace.
28 Aegean fleece.

Did you hear about the couple who met in a revolving door? They're still going around together.

Love Is in the Air

Here's hoping this is a puzzle you'll love to solve!

ACROSS

1 Lovebirds.
3 Touching event.
6 To treasure a treasure.
8 It has a ring to it.
9 It has potential.
10 Knot time.
12 Hitching post?
14 You might see one in a palm.
15 It's often in a text.
17 You can picture it.
19 Heavenly love.
20 Tulips time?
22 Sweet words on a sweet, sometimes. (2 words)
25 You're the judge on how well it floats.
27 "I love you a bunch!"

DOWN

2 "Yes" follower.
3 They're noteworthy.
4 Some might come with flowers.
5 It could be ajar...or to like a lot!
6 Infatuation.
7 Comb go-with.
11 This bud's for you.
13 Tuneful confession. (2 words)
14 One you might fawn over?
16 Light of your life?
18 Main squeeze?
21 "Hmmm...are they an __?"
22 It could be tied...or your admirer!
23 Uniting words. (2 words)
24 Cuddle.
26 Gift from a well-versed swain.

When life is coming
apart at the seams
call a friend who will
keep you in STITCHES

Sew What?

This puzzle could have you in stitches before you know it!

ACROSS

3 It *appears* that these join together.
4 Fingertip cap.
7 A *ribbiting* notion?
9 "Stitch in time" saves them.
10 Your nerves, on occasion?
11 Sample strip.
12 You might cushion them.
16 "__ twice, cut once."
17 Wool under pressure.
19 Some go to pieces over it.
21 What the lounger is doing?
22 Haw's partner.
24 They'll give you fits.
27 What the red, red robin was doing.
28 It's a case for sewing.
29 Don't let it spool you.

DOWN

1 Cloth, espec. for knitting or weaving.
2 Knitter's gem?
5 Warp's partner.
6 Tall tale?
8 It has ups and downs.
9 They've got eyes for you.
13 It's a pressing matter.
14 It's always on edge.
15 Cute simile word.
18 Dancing points? (2 words)
20 They're really snippy.
23 You might favor it.
25 Rat-ta follower.
26 They're often tightly strung.
27 "Make a dash for it!"

I guarantee this computer will do half your work for you.

That's great! I'll take two!

Technology Bytes

This is sure to click with you!

ACROSS

2 Garden home?
3 It gets plugged in.
6 __ Valley, California.
7 Tension connection?
10 "Now I get it!"
12 Don't lose it when you stand up!
14 "Hey, waiter!"
15 Chocolate component?
16 You might file it.
18 Cyber-snack.
19 Cat's pursuit.
21 There's no place like it!
25 Big eater's mouthful.
28 Brainy phone.
30 Bad-words spewer?
31 Door opener.

DOWN

1 Pre-program program.
4 You might be left to your own.
5 Cyan molar?
7 "Uh-oh" go-to.
8 Cyber-chuckle.
9 You know its type.
11 Conversation corner. (2 words)
13 It has a tower.
17 Core machine, for some.
20 "Good catch!"
22 Watch it!
23 Windows shopper?
24 6 Across business.
26 Prepare to walk in snow? (2 words)
27 Key to freedom.
29 Key of choice?

Teacher: "Obviously, you haven't studied your geography. What's your excuse?"
Student: "Well, Dad says the world is changing every day, so I thought I'd wait until it settles down."

Well-Schooled

See how you do with these classy clues!

ACROSS

1 Where students play with notes.
3 It may be technical.
6 School dwelling?
7 He might drill you.
9 They'll research matters.
14 Bibliophile.
15 Pre-elementary school.
17 Content of course.
18 Teachers introduce you to it.
23 School swap?
24 Cyber-school.
28 This school has pull!
29 Higher learning held here.
30 It helps with bills.
31 Tot's school.
32 Hot school?

DOWN

2 Night school subject?
4 Beginning studies.
5 Church-run school.
8 School for overnighters.
10 Pastoral school?
11 "Sounds like..."
12 Cadet's school.
13 It could be lettered.
16 Post-elementary school.
   (2 words)
19 Advice giver.
20 They're often popped.
21 Are you ready for this school?
22 Higher-ups.
25 Grounds for schooling.
26 After-class class.
27 They've been there, done that.

153

God gave us two ears and one mouth
so we could listen
twice as much as we speak.

Shhh!

You might want some peace and quiet while you solve this puzzle.

ACROSS

2 Truth's partner, often.
3 Silence-preserving site.
5 Safe site.
6 Peace core?
10 Balm-y music descriptor.
11 Setting for silence.
14 Shades of peace?
16 Re-pieced peace.
17 Off-time.
19 Absence of effort.
21 Inner-calm system?
25 Peace agreement.
26 Shhh! site, formerly.
27 Sacred speaking.
28 Solo state.
29 Repose result.

DOWN

1 Puppy command?
2 Rest of the day?
4 Piece of your mind?
5 "You won't find me there."
7 Child's imposed quietude, perhaps. (hyph.)
8 Sigh of satisfaction.
9 Grape-growers peace?
12 Cornered quiet.
13 "Sleep in __ peace."
15 Peace-lover's cell phone setting.
17 Tuneful peace?
18 Poised peace?
20 Self-repair?
22 It's still.
23 Freedom from workaday demands.
24 Place to step back.

155

Nan: It's raining cats and dogs today!
Stan: I sure hope it doesn't reindeer tomorrow!

Pun 'n Games

You might develop clue-strophobia with this puzzle!

ACROSS

2 Where love means nothing. (2 words)
9 Horse behind bars.
10 Oak in a nutshell.
11 It's in a pickle.
12 Snowplow driver is sure to get yours.
13 It's often cubed.
14 It gets more sheepish as it grows older.
17 They have a dry sense of humor.
19 This class will give you problems.
20 I-dolatry.
22 Orchestra with no strings attached.
25 Call of the riled.
27 It could be in a teapot.
28 Phony pony. (2 words)
30 Snowman's reputation for being unreliable.

DOWN

1 One who lets nothing go to waist.
3 Give him an inch, and he thinks he's a __.
4 Frenzied rush to the post office.
5 You can count on it.
6 It holds hands.
7 They make light of things.
8 One who's always down to earth.
15 It grows up as it grows down.
16 They make the cut.
18 Soar spot on a slope. (2 words)
21 He'll beat it.
23 It's all keyed up.
24 It might hang by a thread.
26 A sport with many drawbacks.
29 It's worn by the foot.

157

I want to look for my missing watch, but I just can't find the time.

More Pun 'n Games

If you haven't had enough pun-tribulation, here's one more!

ACROSS

1 You might get a charge out of them.
5 Nap sack.
9 Card player's gait.
11 Some are versed in it.
13 You might take it in a pinch.
15 It gets harder with time.
17 It might whistle for you.
18 You can drop them a line.
21 Paper wait?
22 She leaves on a high note.
24 Yell of experience.
26 This teacher has problems.
27 They know the ground rules.
28 Kneady one.
29 Capital of capital. (2 words)

DOWN

2 There's no bones about it.
3 They sale away.
4 Fear of relatives?
6 You might takes steps to avoid it.
7 They might be hard to get over.
8 It has your back.
10 It might have a ring to it.
12 Fast-moving tale.
14 It's a joint concern.
16 They might be drawn.
19 It'll come back to you.
20 It can see right through you. (hyph.)
23 They'll raise the roof.
25 Looking-out glass.
27 Strong adherent.

"Why it was so hot last summer," said the Farmer, "I fed the chickens cracked ice so they wouldn't lay hard-boiled eggs."

Climate Control

Let's see *weather* you can figure out these hot clues!

ACROSS

2 Whiteout!
5 It might shadow you.
6 It comes in streaks.
9 Bursts of swirls.
10 Quick wind.
13 It points in the right direction.
15 Certain woman's bluster?
16 Low-pressure low place.
18 It's beamed down.
20 Windy Indian season.
23 It's gonna be cold, and it's comin' through!
24 Noah's ark arc.
26 Sky blue.
27 One way to get a taxi.
28 Teapot's storm.
29 It might make you misty-eyed.

DOWN

1 Nitty-gritty dirt band.
3 It's tied up with wind speed.
4 It gives you the shivers.
5 Rockies' warm wind.
7 They'll hang tight.
8 Burst of weather.
10 Californian's hot air. (2 words)
11 *Brrrr*-ly guy. (2 words)
12 Rain cloud.
14 It's easy!
17 It makes for a sticky situation.
19 It might have its eye on you.
21 They're hotly discussed every summer. (2 words)
22 It will leave you spinning.
23 It leaves you underwater.
25 Hard rain.

Did you hear about the archaeologist who quit his job? He found his career in ruins.

Let's Work It Out

Make it your business to solve this puzzle! Every answer follows the word "work" or "working."

ACROSS

3 Intern's program, maybe.
4 There might be a monitor there.
6 Some go by it.
8 They do more than mare-ly enough!
9 It's in the bureau.
15 You can picture the plans.
16 You associate with them.
17 M-F, for many.
18 Your boss might change it!
21 Time-out time.
22 Watch it!
23 It's how you operate.
26 Schmoozer's work site. (2 words)
28 You're all in it together.
29 You might tool around in there.
30 It works at work.

DOWN

1 It's your 9-5.
2 Whistle while you work!
3 They can stand you.
5 Telecommuter's preference. (2 words)
7 Company at the company.
10 It knows your agenda.
11 You may be seated.
12 It's where you go.
13 They tell you what to do.
14 CFO's concern.
19 When you take work with you.
20 You might be called on it.
24 You might exercise this option.
25 At first, it's gross.
27 It's a matter of principle.
29 Hard hat area.

Courage is fear that has said its prayers.
Dorothy Bernard

Red, White, and Blue

Maybe you'll flag this puzzle as your favorite!

ACROSS

5 The flag may have left her in stitches. (2 words)
7 Anthem's waver.
8 Stars took over its field. (2 words)
11 Flag waver.
13 Armstrong planted a flag there.
15 Flag defenders.
20 Colonies' flag lines.
22 Stars stand for them.
23 First stars-and-stripes waver.
24 They're presented at ceremonies.
25 Parade flag carriers, often.
26 National flyer.
27 Flag Flyer
28 Flag signal.
29 Thirteenth star. (2 words)

DOWN

1 Anthem opener. (2 words)
2 Key anthem composer. (2 words)
3 Ceremonial flag team. (2 words)
4 Flag Day month
5 Anthem's last word.
6 Stars and Stripes. (2 words)
9 You might put your hand on it.
10 Flag sign of sorrow. (2 words)
12 First flag approver.
14 Fiftieth star.
16 Freedom's day.
17 Flag stands for it.
18 Pledge follower.
19 First star.
21 First American stars.

**Action speaks louder than words,
but not nearly as often.
Mark Twain**

Compound It!

The components of each clue point to a common compound word!

ACROSS

1 Manner of a
   woodworking tool.
6 Celestial shine.
7 Cob's percussion instrument.
8 Sad hat.
9 Yen for what the dog buried.
12 Rod's vertical reading.
13 dwelling's grip.
16 Planet's shiver.
19 Irritate sharply.
21 Watch labor.
22 Corrugated auto.
25 Tab Jill's partner.
26 Essential 2x4.
27 Base butter.
28 Goose feathers theater group.

DOWN

2 Feathered attaché.
3 Limb of a meeting leader.
4 Solid stuff.
5 Concern yourself with liberty.
8 Badge cavity.
10 Earsplitting aperture.
11 Scornful fowl.
12 Shatter quickly!
13 Neigh-sayer with wings.
14 Achieving mailer.
15 Soil swine.
17 Slice skyward.
18 Pre-palm.
20 Zany one's beach find.
21 Dumb-joke zone.
23 Seeing mirror.
24 Post-consequence.

"A bird in the hand is worth two in the bush."
Q: Where did this saying originate?
A: The Bible!

So They Say!

Each clue refers to a well-known proverb or saying.

ACROSS

6 Some sob over it. (2 words)
7 Absence increases its fondness.
8 Moves in mysterious ways.
9 They frolic when felines are far.
10 Purchaser's warning.
11 Rain falls into it. (2 words)
15 Speak thoughtfully, but do this thoroughly.
18 Opening you don't want to step into.
19 Deceiver's weaving accomplishment. (2 words)
23 It's in the observer's eye.
24 Noisy barrel's condition.
25 If it's saved, it's earned.
26 They come to those who wait. (2 words)
28 Clearly, it's a soft pillow.
29 It's beneath the bridge.

DOWN

1 Don't let the sun set on it.
2 Don't evaluate it on its outer layer.
3 Everything glittery isn't it.
4 It's in both palm and bush.
5 Giving compared to getting.
6 Hot-iron action.
12 Contentment is an on-going one.
13 One kindness calls for it.
14 Sole method of gaining friends. (2 words)
16 Each one is double-sided.
17 Shared feature of flocking fowls.
18 It loves company.
20 The proof it there.
21 One in time saves nine.
22 You can't consume it and own it, too.
25 There's nothing achieved without it.
27 You can't do it on bread only.

Optimism:
A cheerful frame of mind that
enables a tea kettle to sing
though in hot water up to its nose.

Positive Thinking

"I know I can, I know I can, I know I can...solve this puzzle!"

ACROSS

4 Mighty thought's might.
6 Positive conviction.
7 Purely positive thoughts.
10 It's a pleasure!
11 Positive thinking makes it.
13 You think funny with it.
15 Your thoughts __ your outlook.
18 You positively __ for the best.
19 You know it!
21 Stadium sound.
24 A positive frame of __ is a good thought!
25 Positive reflection. (hyph.)
28 Moody thoughts?
29 It's what to look on. (2 words)
31 How you think about it is how you see it.
32 Can do, if you think you can.

DOWN

1 Positive thoughts are good for it.
2 "In God we __."
3 Thankfulness.
5 It comes with certain thoughts.
8 You get what you __.
9 Dear thought?
12 Deciding thought.
14 Glass-half-full thinker has it.
16 Think "yes" to you!
17 Positive thoughts invite it.
20 Your thoughts determine how you take it.
22 Many can find one, even in adversity.
23 Thoughtful giver's attribute.
26 Positive greeting.
27 Cozy thoughts bring it to you.
30 Lovely thoughts' source.

PAGE 6/7 SOLUTION

PAGE 8/9 SOLUTION

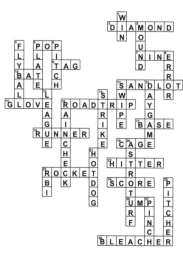

PAGE 10/11 SOLUTION

PAGE 12/13 SOLUTION

PAGE 14/15 SOLUTION

PAGE 16/17 SOLUTION

PAGE 18/19 SOLUTION

PAGE 20/21 SOLUTION

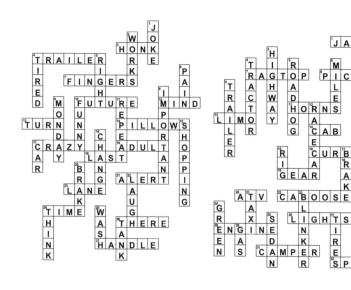

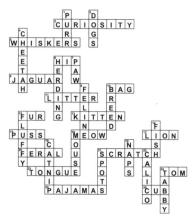

PAGE 30/31 SOLUTION

PAGE 32/33 SOLUTION

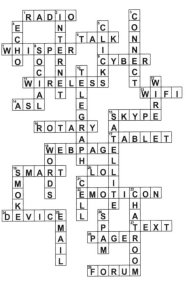

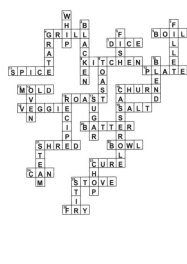

PAGE 34/35 SOLUTION

PAGE 36/37 SOLUTION

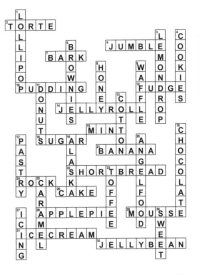

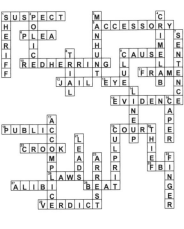

PAGE 38/39 SOLUTION

PAGE 40/41 SOLUTION

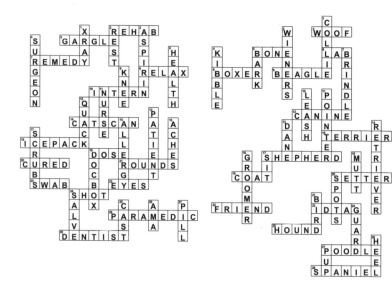

PAGE 42/43 SOLUTION

PAGE 44/45 SOLUTION

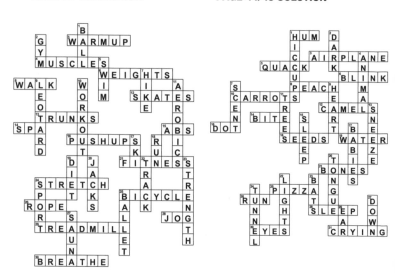

PAGE 46/47 SOLUTION

PAGE 48/49 SOLUTION

PAGE 50/51 SOLUTION

PAGE 52/53 SOLUTION

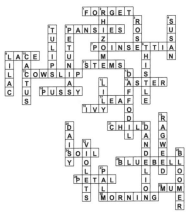

PAGE 54/55 SOLUTION

PAGE 56/57 SOLUTION

PAGE 58/59 SOLUTION

PAGE 60/61 SOLUTION

PAGE 62/63 SOLUTION

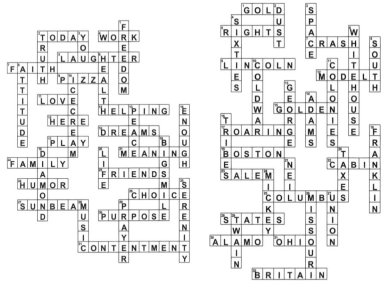

PAGE 64/65 SOLUTION

PAGE 66/67 SOLUTION

PAGE 68/69 SOLUTION

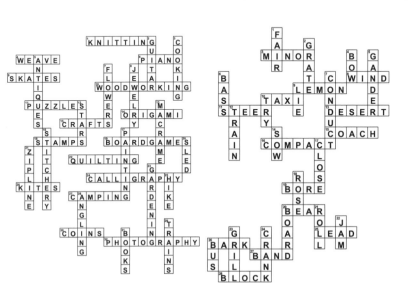

PAGE 70/71 SOLUTION

PAGE 72/73 SOLUTION

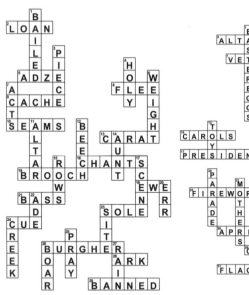

PAGE 74/75 SOLUTION

PAGE 76/77 SOLUTION

PAGE 78/79 SOLUTION

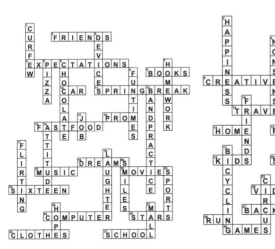

PAGE 80/81 SOLUTION

PAGE 82/83 SOLUTION

PAGE 84/85 SOLUTION

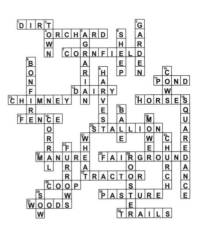

PAGE 86/87 SOLUTION

PAGE 88/89 SOLUTION

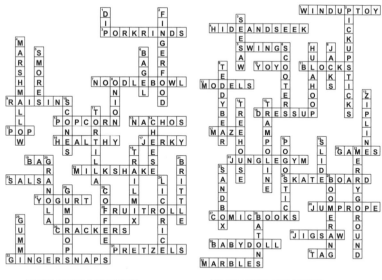

PAGE 90/91 SOLUTION

PAGE 92/93 SOLUTION

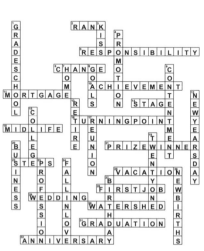

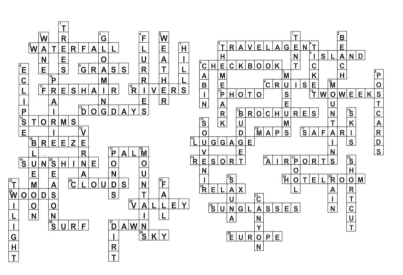

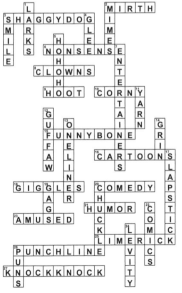

PAGE 102/103 SOLUTION   **PAGE 104/105 SOLUTION**

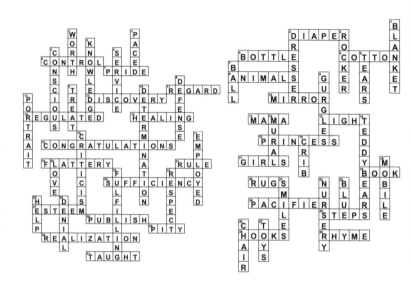

PAGE 106/107 SOLUTION   **PAGE 108/109 SOLUTION**

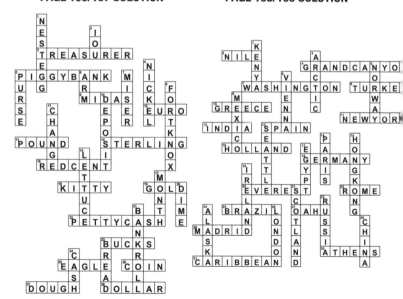

PAGE 110/111 SOLUTION

PAGE 112/113 SOLUTION

PAGE 114/115 SOLUTION

PAGE 116/117 SOLUTION

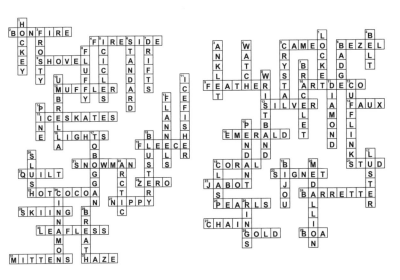

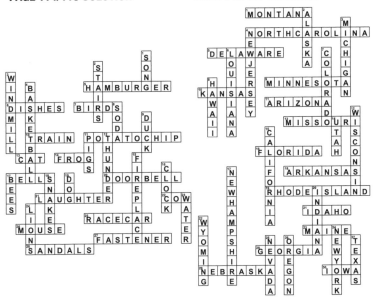

PAGE 118/119 SOLUTION

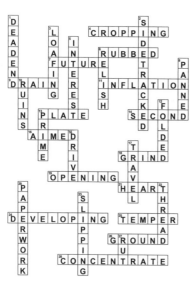

PAGE 120/121 SOLUTION

PAGE 122/123 SOLUTION

PAGE 124/125 SOLUTION

PAGE 126/127 SOLUTION

PAGE 128/129 SOLUTION

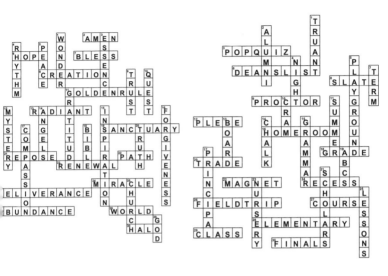

PAGE 130/131 SOLUTION

PAGE 132/133 SOLUTION

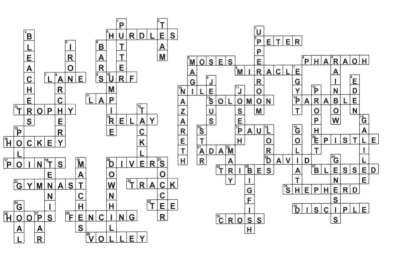

PAGE 134/135 SOLUTION

PAGE 136/137 SOLUTION

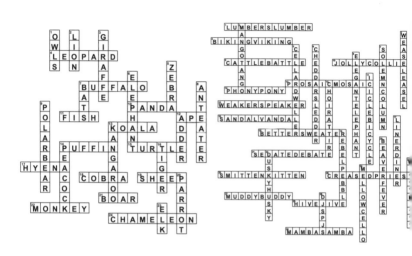

PAGE 138/139 SOLUTION

PAGE 140/141 SOLUTION

PAGE 142/143 SOLUTION

PAGE 144/145 SOLUTION

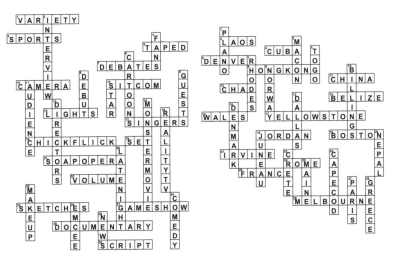

PAGE 146/147 SOLUTION

PAGE 148/149 SOLUTION

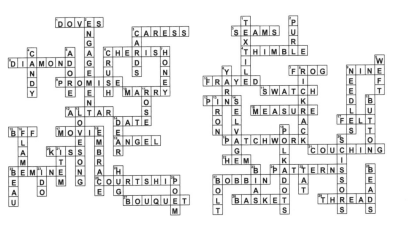

PAGE 150/151 SOLUTION

PAGE 152/153 SOLUTION

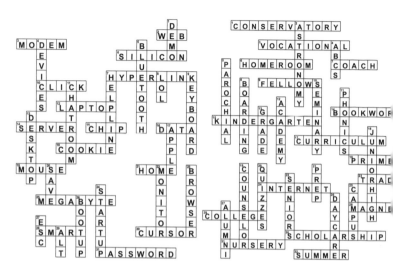

PAGE 154/155 SOLUTION

PAGE 156/157 SOLUTION

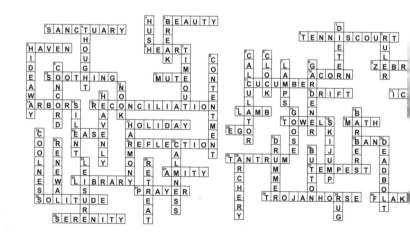

PAGE 158/159 SOLUTION

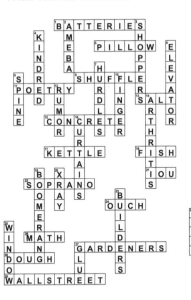

PAGE 160/161 SOLUTION

PAGE 162/163 SOLUTION

PAGE 164/165 SOLUTION

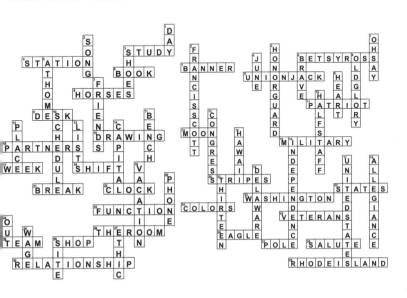

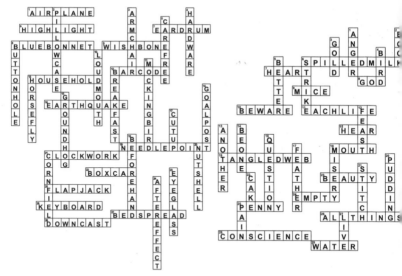

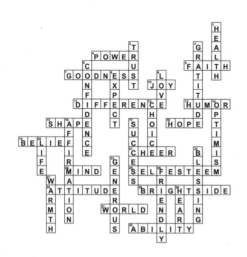

*If you feel like life
is a big puzzle,
Let God help you
piece it together!*